BADGE ON CAMPUS
The Memoir af a School Resource Officer

BADGE ON CAMPUS

The Memoir of a School Resource Officer

Retired Alameda County Sheriff's Deputy
Floyd W. GILL

ABOOKS
Alive Book Publishing

Badge on Campus
Copyright © 2016 by Floyd W. Gill

Additional copies may be ordered from the publisher for educational, business, promotional or premium use. For information, contact ALIVE Book Publishing at: alivebookpublishing.com, or call (925) 837-7303.

Book Design by Alex Johnson
Edited by Sharon McClain Gill

ISBN 13
978-1-63132-031-6

ISBN 10
1-63132-031-9

Library of Congress Control Number: 201694683

Library of Congress Cataloging-in-Publication Data is available upon request.

First Edition

Published in the United States of America
by ALIVE Book Publishing and ALIVE Publishing Group, imprints of Advanced Publishing LLC
3200 A Danville Blvd., Suite 204, Alamo, California 94507
alivebookpublishing.com

PRINTED IN THE UNITED STATES OF AMERICA

10 9 8 7 6 5 4 3 2 1

Foreword

My husband, Floyd W. Gill, is so loved and highly regarded by his former students that we rarely go anywhere without hearing some former student call out to him, "Officer Gill." This happens frequently; at shopping malls, and grocery stores—just about everywhere. They are always happy to see him and they usually reminisce for at least a few minutes, sometimes much longer. We also encounter parents that express their gratitude and appreciation for the help that Floyd provided to their child. And it's not just the students and parents, as school staff are always so happy to see him and tell me what a wonderful man he is. I just say "I Know!"

~ Sharon McClain Gill

Acknowledgments

I want to recognize my fellow Deputies with the Alameda County Sheriff's Office and all assigned to the School Resource Officer's unit.

A special thanks to my friends William Eskridge, L.A. James, Vic Turjanis, Dave Dickson and Ray Lashley. We were the originals SROs that started this successful and unique unit.

Also, a thank you goes out to school administrators, school board members and our many friends with the Castro Valley Unified School District, San Lorenzo Unified School District and the Dublin Unified School District.

Introduction

My career in law enforcement began in 1986 as a Deputy Sheriff with the Alameda County Sheriff's Office. I worked at numerous duty stations since joining the department. In 1991 I was selected as the first School Resource Officer assigned to the Castro Valley Unified School District. My assignment was to help the school districts establish school safety procedures. In 1998, I was transferred to patrol with the City of Dublin. There I was selected as the first School Resource Officer assigned to the Dublin Unified School District.

I was a court certified gang expert and I taught gang topics in the police academy. In 1999, I was offered a position as a part-time teacher for the Tri-Valley Regional Occupation Program in Livermore after I received a California Teaching Credential through San Jose State University. As a teacher for the Tri-Valley Regional Occupation Program I taught Criminal Justice and CSI topics to juniors and seniors as an elective class. I retired from the Alameda County Sheriff's Office on November 01, 2012.

The stories written in this book are true however the accounts were slightly changed due to legal appeals and petitions as well as the actual names of all persons involved. The stories were from calls of service I received while assigned to the Castro Valley Unified School District and the Dublin Unified School District.

The goal of writing this book is to provide a reference for students, parents, school administrators and the general public regarding situations school students are involved in todays public schools.

The California Penal Code section 26 states juveniles cannot be arrested if they are under 14 years of age and lack knowledge of the law or if they lack knowledge of its wrongfulness. I learned that the juvenile justice system was not set up to incarcerate juveniles.

The California juvenile justice system would rather teach, counsel and reprimand juveniles for their misguided behavior and later release them back to their parents or legal guardian once the juveniles were able to demonstrate they leaned a life lessons.

The Juvenile Youth Court is a type of diversion program where juveniles are judged by their peers, sentenced by their peers and counseled by learning and understanding the justice system.

As their School Resource Officer and school liaison I was able to use different forms of teaching techniques to teach the many juveniles a life lesson and reform their actions.

I was successful with many juveniles and unsuccessful with a few that refused to listen and conform their bad behavior. This book is an example of some of my teaching techniques.

Table of Contents

Chapter One

THE CANDY MAFIA

I received a call from Assistant Principal Jessica Walters at Canyon Middle School regarding a child custody issue. Mrs. Walters needed information about a current court proceeding and was preparing to meet with a parent involved in a child custody hearing after our meeting.

I parked my patrol car at the curb in front of the school and began walking to the main office to meet Mrs. Walters. A school bus was unloading students when the driver saw me. The school bus driver called me over.

The school bus driver said, "Officer Gill would you have a conversation with that kid with the red hair. (I noticed she pointed at a student she was referring to) He is always causing problems on my bus. He needs a little scare." I told her I would do it right now and I walked to catch up to the 10-year old boy.

I called out "young man" and he turned around. His eyes went straight to my gun belt and he saw this tall police officer with a gun on his hip. He had a scared look on his face and I said, "I know what you are up to on the school bus!"

He immediately reached into the waistband area of his baggy pants and he handed me a rusty 8" machete (Yes, a machete) he had concealed in his baggy trousers. He told me "I just brought the machete to scare them. "I immediately took the machete away from him and I said, " let's go see Mrs. Walters right now."

I walked the little red head kid past the assistant principal's

13

secretary and we walked into Mrs. Walters's office unan-
nounced. Mrs. Walters was on the telephone and I placed the
machete on her desk. She took a look at it and told the person
on the telephone that she had to go and she just hung up the telephone. I told her how I obtained the machete.

Mrs. Walters said, "Jeffrey, why did you bring a machete to
school today?" that's when Jeffrey really broke down and immediately began to cry.

Little Jeffrey said, "I just wanted my share of the candy." He
went on to tell us how he was a look out as fellow 6th graders
Brian, Mike and Tommy stole candy from the Longs Drug store
every morning before school.

There was a Longs Drug store located on the corner of Castro
Valley Blvd and Marshall Street. The school bus stop was mid-
block on Marshall Street and all students attending middle
school took that bus.

Mrs. Walters told Jeffrey to wait outside her office as she
called his mother. When he left the office Mrs. Walters asked
how we should handle this. I told her that I would secure the
machete in my patrol car and when I returned we could interview Brian, Mike and Tommy.

I asked which student was the weak link and would tell the
truth first. Mrs. Walters immediately told me Brian was the weak
link and that she was sure that he would talk as soon as he entered her office.

When I returned from securing the evidence (the machete)
in my patrol car Brian, Mike and Tommy were sitting outside of
Mrs. Walters's office. They all had scared and nervous looks on
their faces.

Mrs. Walters called the boys into her office and I asked each
boy their names because I wanted to concentrate on Brian.

When Brian announced his name I said, "Brian! So you are
the leader of this group! What do you call your gang, the candy
mafia?" I noticed he had an even more nervous and surprised

look on his face after that comment.

I grabbed a chair and I sat very close to the boys to make their anxiety level rise even more. I asked the boys, "Tell me, how have candy sales been lately?" They all looked at each other and Brian said, "It was Mikes idea to steal the candy, I was just a look out." Soon they all began blaming and pointing the finger at each other.

We learned that every morning the four boys would enter the Longs Drug store and load up their backpacks with candy from the store. After the backpacks were full they would catch their school bus and go to their middle school. The boys would sell the candy at morning breaks and during their lunch periods.

Mrs. Walters told the boys to empty their backpacks on her desk and out fell dozens of Snickers bars, Hershey bars, Three Musketeers bars and candy bars I never saw before. They told us the reason they stole the candy was that they were going to buy karate uniforms and martial arts videos with their profits.

I told them as of now they are officially out of business. I asked them how long have they been stealing the candy from the drug store and how much money they had collected. I was told they had over $400. Mrs. Walters told the boys she was very disappointed in them and she began calling their parents. They just sat there crying.

When I met up with the parents we came up with a plan to repay their debt. The plans called for each of them to each take $100 and return it to the drug store to pay their debt. Each boy had to meet up with the store manager and hand him a letter of apology for stealing from the store. Then they were told not to return inside the store for anything for the remainder of the school year.

I told the boys that there were cameras behind the two-way mirrors inside the store. I told them that I would check with the store manager every week to make sure they kept their word. I ended saying if I saw them inside the store on camera the deal was off and they would all be in trouble all over again. I told the boys there were video cameras inside the store so they would not return to the store to harass store employees or customers as some type of revenge.

All the boys were suspended from school for stealing candy. Jeffrey was suspended for possession of a machete and he too was told not to enter the store for the remainder of the school year.

I had to quickly drive to the Long's drug store to inform the store manager that four kids were coming in with their parents to pay for all the candy they stole. The store manager said. "I thought candy sales were good all month."I told the manager to just accept their money, accept their letters of apology and let them go home with their parents.

About two weeks later I was on the service road behind the drug store checking for graffiti. Every Monday morning I would always drive behind businesses around town to check for graffiti vandalism. As I slowly drove on the service road behind the drug store, the store manager flagged me down.

The store manager asked, "How many kids were coming in to pay for stolen merchandise?" I thought to myself, I hope the parents did what they promised to do and pay for the stolen candy.

My reply was four 6th graders and their parents. The store manager said, "So far about eleven kids, mostly girls, were paying for merchandise they stole from the store." The girls were paying for make-up and cosmetics they stole from the store cosmetics department.

The manager said, "They all think there is a video camera behind the two-way mirrors." I left after telling the store manager not to tell them otherwise and your theft problem will come to an end.

Another big case solved by great school administrators, involved parents, good community policing and the SRO.

Chapter Two

ALWAYS KEEP
YOUR WORDS SWEET

It was Tuesday, April 20, 1999, and a very sad day in American History. On that day around 11:19 am Colorado time two students, 17 year old Dylan Klebold and 18 year old Eric Harris, went on a killing spree at Columbine High School in Littleton, Colorado. On that day Dylan Klebold and Eric Harris murdered 12 students and one teacher. They also injured an additional 21 students during their killing spree that ended around 12:10 pm Central Standard time.

The breaking news broadcast was around 12:30 pm Colorado time and 11:30 am Pacific Standard time. Every news channel in America was covering the sad outcome of that day.

A Dublin High School teacher that once taught high school in Colorado decided to tune on the live CNN news coverage of the event. His students were in class watching the breaking news event live from Colorado on their Dublin High School classroom TV.

Sitting in the back of the classroom was Barry. Many students considered Barry a loner type student that did not have many friends that shared his same interests. Barry spent many hours on his home computer playing computer war games.

As the CNN news reporter described the events unfolding live on camera Barry would mention the names of the shooters. Barry sitting in the rear of the classroom would confirm the reporter's statements by saying "that's my friends Dylan Klebold and Eric Harris."

Students watching the news overheard Barry comments. The students would look at each other and whisper during Barry's comments. Barry went on to say his friends Dylan and Eric were members of the "Trench Coat Mafia".

As the reporter read from his notes he would say on camera that Dylan Klebold and Eric Harris were members of a group calling themselves the Trench Coat Mafia. Now the students would again whisper and look at Barry. Some of the students in the classroom wondered how did Barry know about the Trench Coat Mafia? Are Dylan Klebold and Eric Harris really friends of Barry's?

Barry watched and continued to comment before the news reporter spoke on camera. Barry said his friends Dylan Klebold and Eric Harris did not like the "Jocks" (student athletes) because the jocks always bullied and harassed them at school. And once again the news reported gave a possible cause for the shooting as retaliation against the student athletics or jocks at school because of the jocks harassment towards Dylan Klebold and Eric Harris.

Students sitting in the classroom began to look at Barry and wonder if they were in trouble because some of school jocks harassed Barry on occasion.

It did not take long but the school rumor mill began to spread the word about Barry. Who was Barry? You know that strange kid that sits in the back of the classroom. Did you hear Barry is a friend of those weird kids that killed a bunch of kids in Colorado? You know the Trench Coat Mafia kids. Oh that Barry.

It was 12:05 pm in Dublin and now the high school lunch period began. Barry would often sit by himself in the school library during the lunch period but now all students were watching Barry. He could feel all the eyes and the sudden attention he was getting. He could see a lot of students whispering as he walked through the campus.

Before Barry entered the school library a group of girls approached him. The girls had a question for Barry but only one girl had the courage to ask the question all the students wanted to know.

The girl, with her two friends standing by her side, asked Barry, "Are you going to shoot us like your friends in Colorado did?"

Barry gave a sarcastic answer saying, "Yes! Yes! I plan on shooting all of you! Now leave me alone!"

That was the wrong answer.

The girls called their parents at work in a panic. The girls all wanted to leave campus and go home now because they made the quiet loner Barry angry.

Suddenly the school attendance clerk had numerous angry parents on campus withdrawing their children from class. The reason given for the withdrawal was a student on campus was going to shoot students like the shooting that occurred in Colorado.

The attendance clerks called the principal and informed her of what was occurring in the attendance office. There was a panic on campus as some students just walked off campus without going to class.

That's when I received a call on my cellphone from Dublin High School Principal Mary Evans. She informed me she needed me on campus immediately. I was on campus in less than four minutes. I reported to the principal's office to collect information on her call for police service.

In Principal Evans office was Assistant Principal Dave Marks and 10th grade student Barry. Principal Evans asked if I parked my patrol car in front of the school and I said "Yes". She said, "Good because it may calm things on campus right now". I asked what the problem was.

Principal Evans informed me that Barry came to their attention through students and very angry and concerned parents. I learned about Barry's classroom comments during the live CNN report on the Columbine High School shooting and Barry's comments during the school lunch period.

Assistant Principal Marks informed me that Barry was a friend of Columbine High School shooters Dylan Klebold and Eric Harris and that Barry communicated with the shooters before the Colorado school shooting took place today.

I looked at Barry and asked, "Is all this information being told to me true?" and Barry answered "Yes, I would exchange images and games with Eric Harris on my home computer all the time". I then asked Barry "Did you tell a group of girls that you were going to shoot them" and Barry said, "Yeah, I just wanted them to leave me alone".

I told Barry that I had probable cause to detain him to investigate his actions and his involvement in disrupting the school campus by making threats to harm other students on campus and his involvement in the current shooting in Colorado.

I informed Principal Evans that I was going to transport Barry to the police station for additional information on his computer conversations with the Columbine shooters and that I was gong to contact my friends with the FBI to assist me with my investigation.

Assistant Principal Marks told me that Barry's mother worked for the Dublin school district and that he would contact her at the school job site regarding her son.

Principal Evans suspended Barry for making threats to kill the female students and for causing a major disruption on the campus by his angry comments.

Principal Evans said she was going to contact the school district's superintendent and inform him of all the events that occurred at the high school.

I transported Barry to the police station and contacted the Chief of Police through the chain of command. Everyone at the police station saw Barry and thought Barry did not look like a threat to anyone.

Less that fifteen minutes later two FBI agents arrived at the Dublin Police Station. I informed FBI Special Agent Johnson and Special Agent Jackson that Barry admitted to communicating with Columbine High School shooters Dylan Klebold and Eric Harris on his home computer and today he admitted to telling students at Dublin High School that he was going to shoot them like the Columbine Colorado shooters did.

The FBI agents wanted to see Barry's home computer to get an idea on how involved Barry was with the Columbine school shooters.We all drove over to Barry's home to collect his personal computer.

When we arrived, Barry's mother Marjorie was at home waiting for us. When Barry walked into his home she immediately began to hug him and cry as she held him. Marjorie told us the superintendent informed her about what occurred at Dublin High School.

I introduced Marjorie to the FBI agents and I told her that they were at her home asking for her permission to collect her son's home computer. Marjorie allowed them to take Barry's computer, as she wanted to assist us with our investigation.

Just before we left Barry's home with his computer I received a cell phone call from Principal Evans. She wanted us to know that several news crews were around the Dublin campus asking about what occurred on campus earlier.

Principal Evans referred all the TV news and press reporters to the Dublin superintendent's office for an official press statement. I called the police station and informed them that the press was looking for a news story and to get the PIO (Public Information Officer) ready to meet the news reporters.

Marjorie and Barry were very cooperative with the FBI investigation and there were no school discipline or negative police contacts against Barry. I did not see Marjorie or Barry as a danger to the community or a flight risk from justice.

As I was leaving Barry and Marjorie I gave Barry some advice that my grandmother gave me when I was a little boy. My grandmother told me many times, "Always keep your words sweet. Just in case you have to eat them" or she would tell me "If you don't have anything good to say to people, just don't say anything." I was very young and I did not understand what she meant at the time but now I understand.

We learned later at the end of the school day that a news reporter and a camera crew were in Dublin asking students leaving the campus if they knew about the incident at their high school earlier in the day. Several students told reporters that they heard about a student that wanted to kill a girl on campus and that he had a bunch of guns to kill a lot of students. (Not true because Barry did not own any firearms and he did not say he was coming to school with guns) One student told the news reporter where Barry lived with his mother. (True, a couple of students directed news crews towards Barry's home). Later that day Marjorie and Barry noticed a news crew van on their street headed to their home.

Later that afternoon I received a telephone call from the FBI informing me that there was no evidence on Barry's personal home computer indicating he knew of any plot to kill students at Columbine High School in Colorado.

The FBI said that Barry played a computer game that Eric Harris created on his private America Online website. The website offered a computer war game created by Eric Harris that was similar to the video game Doom. The website also included jokes, a short journal entry with thoughts on parents, school cliques, other video games and friends at his school in Colorado.

Barry had a brief conversation with Eric Harris two days prior to the school massacre. The conversation was general thoughts about school events. The FBI retuned Barry's personal computer to me soon after our telephone conversation.

About five days later the school superintendent recommended a special expulsion-hearing panel against Barry for his angry outburst on campus. The special school panel held their hearing to determine if all the information on Barry's disciplinary suspension was serious enough to warrant an expulsion. I was called as a participant in the special school panel hearing.

I informed Barry and his mother Marjorie that I would not testify for Barry or against Barry. I was only there to testify that I was called to the campus by the principal and that a police report was taken to document the incident. Because the case was pending before Juvenile Court the school board was not entitled to a copy of the police report and that was why I was needed before the school board hearing.

After the special administrative hearing the panel chairperson referred Barry's case to the five-member school board because his words or actions caused a major disruption on campus.

The school board agreed with the special panel and investigation and they decided to expel Barry. Unanimously they decided not to allow Barry to attend any school in the Dublin Unified School District for one year.

Barry and Marjorie were very disappointed in the school boards decision but they had a lot of support from some friends, parents and a couple of elementary school principals.

At the end of all the weeks of press coverage regarding the Columbine school shooting I was added to the FBI and Secret Service list for the Columbine High School shootings debriefs and student shooter profiling. The shooter debrief gave a lot of good information about the Columbine shooting that was not covered in public newspapers.

For example, Dylan Klebold and Eric Harris gave a lot of important danger signs and no one took action to immediately check out their threats.

The investigation revealed that Klebold and Harris planned the Columbine school attack for over a year. People that knew and hung around with Dylan Klebold and Eric Harris overheard the threats but they did not report the threats to anyone.

Eric Harris wrote many blurbs on his home computer about his general hatred of society. He made many violent threats against students and teachers at Columbine High School and expressed his desire to kill those who annoyed him. (Just your average teenage psychopathic behavior).

Both Klebold and Harris were on Juvenile Probation for breaking into a neighbors van and their probation officer recommended their early release because of their positive actions. They fooled a lot of people into thinking they were victims of school harassment.

Eric Harris had to attend anger management classes that he sometimes did not make and Dylan Klebold had a history of drinking and he failed a dilute urine test.

Klebold and Harris made over one hundred pipe bombs with CO_2 canisters in a basement and not one adult went downstairs to check on what they were working on. Harris would often brag online about his ability to make bombs and he and Klebold would go into the woods to discharge their bombs to test them. No adults ever checked on what projects they were working on in the basement.

Harris and Klebold kept a journal documenting their arsenal with videotapes they kept hidden. Their journals documented their plan for a major bombing at their school and they mentioned hijacking a plane at Denver International Airport and crashing the plane into buildings in New York City as well as details about their planned attack on Columbine High School. We now know that their journals were a blueprint for the Columbine High School massacre. (Could the 9/11 terrorists get their airplane hijacking idea from a couple of American high school kids?)

Dylan Klebold and Eric Harris were big fans of the movie "Natural Born Killers" and they played a shoot and kill video game for hours daily, possibly as a rehearsal plan for the school massacre. We now know their plan was well thought out due to all the hours playing violent video games.

The FBI profiling information indicated Eric Harris was a clinical psychopath and Dylan Klebold was depressive and they believe Harris had been the mastermind. The FBI class was very helpful and I used some of the information given in the profiling class to recognize some signs, even though not all danger signs can be detected. With this information I learned, I was lucky enough to stop three other possible school shooting incidents during my career.

Later I attended additional classes made available and sponsored by the California Attorney General's Office and the US Department of Juvenile Justice. The classes were for School Resource Officers and school administrators to help recognize troubled students by recognizing their patterns and possible problems. The goal was to help the troubled student and prevent violence on campus.

In May 2002, the Secret Service published a report that examined several school shootings. They listed the following findings in their detailed report.

- Incidents of targeted violence at school were rarely sudden, impulsive acts
- Prior to most incidents, other people knew about the attackers idea and/or plan to attack
- Most attackers did not threaten their targets directly prior to advancing the attack
- There is no accurate or useful profile of students who engaged in targeting school violence
- Most attackers engaged in some behavior prior to the incident that caused others concern or indicated a need for help
- Most attackers had difficulty coping with significant losses or personal failures and many considered or attempted suicide
- Many attackers felt bullied, persecuted or injured by

others prior to attack

- In some cases other students were involved in some capacity
- Despite prompt law enforcement response most shooting incidents were stopped by means other than law enforcement

A lot of lessons were learned after the Columbine High School massacre from police response to new school district policies.

School districts all over America began to address school bullying and the link between bullying and school violence. Early stories reported by the press charged the administrators and teachers at Columbine had long condoned a climate of bullying by the so-called jocks or atheletes allowing an atmosphere of intimidation and resentment toward authorities.

School districts that I was assigned to did a great job of addressing bullying with very strict policies and rules of discipline. I've worked with school administrators that would immediately address school bullying and parents were notified of their child's unacceptable behavior both on and off campus.

As police, we learned not to wait for back up officers and to not waste time setting up perimeters around schools during an active shooter call. We would practice to charge towards the active shooter, locate and stop the shooting threat.

As a School Resource Officer I found some students are often cruel to each other with words and they fail to see that their words can cut like a knife whenever they are angry at each other. Whenever I lectured students at schools about bullying each other I would often end my lecture with my grandmother's wise words.

Personally I do not like watching all situation comedies on TV or in movies where young people cut each other down with canned laughter in the background. I believe some young people watch and learn how to behave from this type of communications and they may not realize that not everyone may see their personal situations as amusing or funny.

America learned a lot from the Columbine High School massacre of April 20, 1999 and we are still learning to make our schools safe.

Let's all keep our words sweet because we may have to eat them one day and it may help us avoid arrest.

Chapter Three

TRUE CONFESSIONS

I received a call from Assistant Principal Steve Martin at Wells Middle School regarding a student he was detaining and suspected of theft from the school. Jessie, a 7th grader, was suspected of taking a video camera from his classroom. Jessie's teacher noticed the camera was missing right after Jessie left the classroom and the teacher wrote his observations on a referral form for Mr. Martin to investigate.

I met with Mr. Martin and 7th grader Jessie in the main office. Mr. Martin told me in private that Jessie was a hard case and that he would never admit to any crimes he was suspected of-committing.

Mr. Martin also told me Jessie's mother always backed her son's claim of innocence no matter what he was accused of and that she would go on a tirade accusing him of being racist and anti-Hispanic. Jessie's mother claimed the school district wanted her son off the campus by always making up false claims of classroom disruptions, bullying or theft against her son.

I met with Jessie and I asked him if the video camera was in his room at home. Jessie responded with a cocky "You don't know that I have the camera and you can't prove that I took the camera!"

I told Jessie that I could prove he had the stolen camera because I have fingerprints. I told Jessie that I'd go out to my patrol car and show him fingerprints. I also told him when you see the evidence I have "I'm going to take you straight to juvenile hall."

I left with Mr. Martin and Jessie waiting for me in the office and walked out to my patrol car. I opened the trunk to my patrol car and I opened my evidence kit. I took out a strip of fingerprint tape and placed my right pinky finger on the tape followed by placing my left pinky finger on the other end of the fingerprint tape. I took out an evidence card and placed the fingerprints on the card. I then used a marker to write Jessie's name under the evidence title on the card. I placed the evidence card in a large evidence envelope. On the other side of the envelope I wrote in large bold print the words fingerprints and DNA evidence.(The law allows police to trick suspects)

I walked back into Mr. Martin's office and I held the evidence envelope up showing Jessie's name on the envelope. Jessie's eyes shot open like a cartoon character.

He dropped his head and he looked down at his own finger-prints on his hands. I told Jessie "Now I'm going to get a search warrant to search your room where I will find the stolen video camera and that dirty magazine under your mattress."

Jessie was choking back his tears and said, "Yes, the video camera is on a dresser in my room but the dirty magazine is hidden in my closet."

Mr. Martin sat there and just smiled. I finally got a confession from Jessie. This was the first time Jessie had ever admitted to doing anything wrong. Jessie had been in Mr. Martin's office many times and he never ever admitted to any wrong doing. Mr. Martin now had something to tell Jessie's mother. That was a phone call he enjoyed making.

Jessie's mother was contacted and told to bring the stolen video camera back to school and to meet with us for a special conference to discuss her son's suspension from school.

About ten minutes later Jessie's mother was on campus with the stolen video camera and a new attitude towards Mr. Martin.

Jessie did not look at his mother when she arrived. We told

her of the teacher's referral and investigation and how Jessie came to our attention. Mr. Martin suspended Jessie and his mother made him apologize.

I told Jessie that his punishment would be special weed abatement. This was a punishment I often used to teach juveniles a lesson. I preferred working juveniles rather than send them to juvenile court.

Jessie's father is a gardener. I told Jessie to have his father show him the difference between a weed and a flower. Jessie was to pull only weeds. Then every day he would take a quick lunch and pull weeds along the fence around the perimeter of the schoolyard. I wanted all the students to see Jessie work off his crime so that they all knew it was wrong to steal and that crime does not pay.

Mr. Martin wanted to know how I managed to get Jessie's fingerprints. I told him, "All I said to Jessie was 'I had fingerprints' because we all have fingerprints. I did not tell Jessie I had his fingerprints."

Mr. Martin laughed and said that was very clever and you finally got Jessie to admit to doing something wrong. The best part was showing his mother that little Jessie was not perfect and his word couldn't be trusted.

I suggested to Mr. Martin that we take a look at what Jessie videotaped with the stolen camera. We took a look at the video and we saw Jessie and two other juveniles smoking cigarettes and drinking beer. We also saw them spray painting gang graffiti on a building.

Mr. Martin called Jessie's mother again to see his video production. She returned with Jessie and she was allowed to see our video evidence.

Jessie's mother was a broken spirit because she saw that her little boy was not as innocent as she assumed. She identified the two unknown juveniles with Jessie as cousins that lived in the City of Oakland.

I called Oakland Police and gave them a copy of our video-tape so they could further investigate the gang and graffiti crime in their city.

I gave Jessie's mother the name and number for family counseling so that the family could get Jessie back on the right track and away from the gang lifestyle.

Jessie's mother was open to allow her son to perform a community service project to repay his debt of wasted time to the school district and the city. I informed her that the City of Dublin was always looking for volunteers during the St. Patrick's Day weekend as the city held a parade and a street fair that was open to the public. I told her that Jessie could work in the Dublin Police Crime Prevention booth as our volunteer. The agreement was made for Jessie's future.

About two weeks later it was St. Patrick's Day and the festival was held in the Dublin City Hall area. Dublin Police had a Crime Prevention booth in the center of the festival. Jessie was there in the booth right on time to volunteer as agreed. Jessie was eager to help but we had a small problem. The problem was the volunteer that agreed to wear the "McGruff the Crime Fighting Dog" costume was sick and could not attend the festival. Jessie was tall and I thought he would fit in the costume.

I said to Jessie that kids at the festival were looking for McGruff the crime fighting dog so he needed to get into the costume. At first he did not want to do it but I reminded him that he volunteered. I said, "Jessie! Get into the costume, kids are waiting". Jessie was sent to a private room and after a couple of minutes he walked out wearing the McGruff costume.

I told Jessie he did not have to say anything but just wave at little kids. Another officer and I walked with Jessie and we handed out coloring books, crayons and colorful stickers for bicycles, pencils and pencil erasers to little kids. At the end of the festival Jessie told me he had a surprisingly good time because I bought him lunch, gave him breaks and I treated him fair. All this made him feel good to help the community and help little kids.

I left the school knowing the SRO solved another hard to solve case.

Chapter Four

THE TURKEY HUNT

On the same block and outskirts of the Castro Valley High School campus there was a small strip mall with a convenience store. In addition to the convenience store the strip mall had a women's beauty salon and a travel agency on the lower level. On the upper level there was an insurance agency, a book keeping service and a janitorial service.

The convenience store was very active during the schools lunch period. When the lunch period bell rang students would just walk across the school's football field and the students parking lot and now they could enjoy a junk food lunch. The parking lot was full of students eating lunch and littering the parking lot.

During my daily patrol I noticed a large group of young adults interacting with the high school students. They drove to the convenience store in their used beat up cars and parked in front of the store taking up a lot of parking spaces in the strip mall. I thought this was odd for all those young unemployed adults to be loitering around the convenience store during the high school lunch period.

I'm an old fashion street cop that once worked an active beat with a lot of drug activities and I knew stoners or dopers (drug abusers) when I saw them. I knew I was looking at a lot of dopers loitering around high school students and I did not like what I was seeing.

About ten minutes before the lunch period was to end I

would announce to all the students, "About ten minutes before lunch will end." Students would hear that announcement and begin walking back to school.

All the adults loitering with the students would laugh saying, "Listen to the kindergarten cop kids and go back to school now" or sometimes they would say, "Yeah, listen to the kiddy cop and don't be late now". I did not like adults loitering with students and I wanted to do something about them.

I recognized one of the students at the convenience store as the son of a police officer. I knew his mom and dad, as they were both police officers. I had been to his house numerous times and I was very familiar with him and his family.

When I returned to my office on campus I sent for him. I asked him the names of all the adults that like to loiter at the convenience store during the lunch period.

Student Monty was very helpful and he gave me the names of many of the adults and the reason why they just happen to loiter around the convenience store every school day. The reason was just what I thought they were doing. All the adults were drug abusers and some were drug dealers. I thought to myself, "Now I have to do something to get rid of these non-students and stop them from hanging around the convenience store during lunch period."

I met with Assistant Principal Jerry White to inquire about all the adult non-students that were loitering during lunch.

When I gave Mr. White some of the names I collected I got an ear full of bad news. Mr. White knew five of the names on the list as former Castro Valley and Redwood Continuation High School students.

Mr. White told me the five former students were involved in fights, bullying, suspected of abusing illegal drugs, selling illegal drugs on campus and miscellaneous disruptions. None of the news about the non-students was good.

I told Mr. White I would have to discourage all the former

36

students from hanging around the convenience store during the lunch period.

Mr. White asked, "How are you going to do that all by yourself?"

I said, "I grew up in Texas and I'll just have to go on a turkey hunt."

Mr. White had a curious look on his face and he asked, "A turkey hunt?"

I explained my turkey hunt comment. When I lived in Texas we would go out to hunt wild turkeys. We would see the turkeys walking towards us in a line.

The secret is to shoot the turkey walking at the end of the line. Turkeys are so stupid they will hear the gunshot but they would not know what to do. They would only look around and look at each other and maybe even scatter for a minute but they would only look ahead and not behind them.

After a couple of seconds they would continue to walk towards us in a line. We would continue to shoot the turkey at the end of the line and again they would stop and hunker down but they would continue to walk towards us in a line. After a couple of seconds they again would walk in a line until they were all shot.

We would share our catch with all our neighbors and friends and we all had wild turkey for dinner. That's a good turkey hunt.

I told Mr. White I will have to come up with a plan for a good turkey hunt starting Monday during the lunch period.

By Monday's school lunch period I had a plan. It was time to start the turkey hunt. I had to remain calm and very patient in order for the hunt to be successful.

Day One- Monday: I drove over to the convenience store and I parked my patrol car where I could see all the non-students as they arrived for the lunch period. There was a tree in the corner of the convenience store parking lot and I parked under the tree in the shade. It was a good spot to observe the entire parking lot and read my copy of the California Vehicle Code.

I watched five to six old beat up looking cars park in front of the store and watched all the adult non-students climb out of their cars. Some went inside the convenience store to purchase bottles of soda or juice. I sat in my parked patrol car and I would watch them line up on the sidewalk slowly sipping their cold drinks. I sat there patiently watching them like a good turkey hunter.

They would look and point at me as I sat in the parking lot watching them. Whenever I would look at the non-students standing on the sidewalk I would give them a smirk of a smile. (gobble gobble)

The lunch bell rang and soon students were in the convenience store to buy their junk food lunches. I would see the non-students interacting with the students and every now and then I would hear them laugh. They had a cocky swagger when they walked along the sidewalk.

I made the announcement and told the students that lunch would end in about ten minutes. A couple of adult non-students would mock me and repeat, "Yeah, you kids don't want to be late for class or the kindergarten cop here will give you detention".

I watched the students return to campus and I watched all the non-students slowly return to their old beat up cars. They began to leave the convenience store parking lot one after another. Now it's time to start the turkey hunt.

I just happened to want to leave the parking lot as well and I would follow behind the last car filled with non-students. Once the car was on the public street I would activate my red and blue emergency lights followed by a short siren blast. The car would pull over to the curb.

I approached the driver and the first thing he said was, "What's the matter kindergarten cop, do you want to see my hall pass?" the passengers in the back seat had a laugh at the drivers joke.

I said, "No, but I would like to see your California drivers license, your car registration and your current proof of auto insurance".

The driver identified himself as Lester and he asked, "Why, you don't have anything else to do right now?"

I said, "Oh yes, I have something to do but first I am going to give you a fix-it ticket for your cracked windshield". Lester replied, "Oh come on, is that the best you can do right now?"

I quoted California Vehicle Code 26710(b) and I told Lester that a cracked windshield had to be repaired within 72 hours of the window being damaged. Lester's passengers gave me a nervous laugh and I heard one passenger say "Oh come on, get real kiddy cop". As you and I know driving around with a cracked windshield is a flagrant violation of state law.

I took notice of Lester's passengers and I saw that they all were not wearing their seat belts. I told all the passengers that I needed their ID's as well as I was going to issue citations to all of them for not wearing their state required seat belts under California Vehicle Code 27315. Once again as you and I know driving around without seat belts is dangerous and another flagrant violation of state law.

After collecting their ID's I returned to my patrol car and began writing citations. The passengers were identified as front seat passenger Clifford and rear seat passengers Nate, Taylor and Lewis.

At the same time I wrote out their citations radio dispatchers informed me that Lester did not have a valid drivers license. Lester's California drivers license was suspended due to a DUI arrest over a year earlier violating California Vehicle Code 14601.

Radio dispatcher also informed me that passenger Nate had an outstanding warrant for his arrest for a drug violation under California Health and Safety Code 11357(d) marijuana possession. Now it was time to enforce justice. I called out driver Lester first.

I had Lester sign his fix-it ticket for the cracked windshield with an additional violation for not having current auto insurance. I noticed the expired auto insurance policy as I wrote the fix-it ticket for the windshield. After Lester signed the citation I placed Lester under arrest for driving on a suspended drivers license. I informed Lester that I had watched him drive to the convenient store several times and until today I did not know he was illegally driving a car on a suspended driver's license.

I placed Lester in handcuffs and sat him in the back seat of my patrol car. I noticed Lester's passengers looking at me as I put the handcuffs on. They had a very nervous look on their faces.

I walked over to the car and called passenger Nate out of the car. I issued Nate a citation for not wearing his seat belt. Nate signed his citation and I informed Nate that he had an outstanding warrant for his arrest.

I placed handcuffs on Nate and I sat him in the back seat of my patrol car with Lester. I took a look at the car and I noticed the remaining three passengers had an even more nervous look on their faces.

Next I called passengers Clifford then Taylor and finally Lewis out of the car one at a time and I issued each one a citation for not wearing their seat belts.

Clifford wanted to drive Lester's car away and I told him that Lester's auto insurance had expired and that he could not drive the car away until he could show me proof of current auto insurance under California Vehicle Code 4000(a).

I gave them a choice to either walk home or run home but they were not going to drive home. They decided to quickly walk home.

I requested a tow truck to remove Lester's car from the road. Because Lester was driving on a suspended drivers license an automatic 30-day storage hold was placed on the car under California Vehicle Code 22651(h) towing authority.

After the tow truck removed Lester's car I transported Lester and Nate to jail. Five citations issued, two stoners going to jail and one car towed away.

I was having a good day because it was a good first day of the turkey hunt.

Day Two- Tuesday: I returned to my spot under the tree in the convenience store parking lot to again read the California Vehicle Code.

I noticed five old beat up looking cars entering the parking lot and parking in the convenience store parking lot. The occupants climbed out of their cars and they looked at me just sitting in my spot. They had an angry look on their faces and I just gave them a smirk.

They went inside the convenience store and again they stood outside on the sidewalk in front of the store with their soda purchases.

The lunch bell rang and students went inside the convenience store to buy their lunch. The non-students intermingled with the high school students as they did the day before.

As before I made the announcement to the students that lunch was ending in about ten minutes. The adult non-students mocked me again and they had a little chuckle as they did the day before.

After the students returned to campus I watched the non-students return to their cars. I watched them drive through the convenience store parking lot and I just happened to follow the last car.

When the car entered the public street I just happened to notice the driver made a left turn without using his turn signal. As you and I know that is a flagrant violation of state law under California Vehicle Code section 22108.

I activated my blue and red emergency lights followed by a

short siren blast. The car pulled over to the shoulder of the road. As I approached the waiting car I noticed the car tires were worn down so low that I could see the metal tread sticking out of the rubber tire, a violation of California Vehicle Code 27465(b).

The driver identified himself as Clay. He was angry and he wanted to know why I pulled him over. I told Clay that he did not use his turn signal indicator as required by California Vehicle Code 22108 when he made his left turn and once I approached his stopped car I noticed his tires were worn down so low that his car was considered unsafe for travel.

Clay said, "Oh come on, no one ever uses their turn signals. There's murderers and rapist out there and you stop me for a turn signal?" I responded saying, "Do you know of a murder or rape you want to report?" Clay said, "No" and I said, "I don't see everyone but, I did see you and you failed to follow state law so until there is a murder or a rape, I'll just focus on you right now". I ended by requesting to see Clays' valid California drivers license, his auto registration and his current proof of auto insurance.

Clay cursed the entire time but he opened his glove box and he took out the paper work that I requested. He handed the papers to me. I informed Clay that I was going to issue him a fix-it ticket for each bald tire and for not using his turn signal when he made his left turn.

I asked the passenger if any of them were on probation or parole and passenger Josh and Marshall admitted they were on court probation for a drug arrest and drug violations under Health and Safety Code 11359-Marijuana Sales.

Because Josh and Marshall were on active court probation for drug violations I requested back up in order to conduct a car search.

As I waited for back up I requested through radio dispatcher to check the driving status on Clay. Dispatchers informed me that Clay did not have a valid drivers license. That was a violation of California Vehicle Code 14601. Did Clay lie to the police because his driver's license is not valid?

Josh and Marshall were confirmed to be on active court probation with a court ordered search clause. The search clause allowed any police office to search them, day or night, with or without an arrest warrant because they were convicted of drug sales crimes.

When back up Deputy Cramer arrived I informed them that I planned on searching Clay's car because I saw the rear passengers Josh and Marshall moving suspiciously during the car stop. Could one of the passengers be attempting to conceal illegal drugs?

I searched the rear passenger compartment first and between the rear seat and rear seat backrest I discovered a small plastic bag filled with a green leafy substance that looked like dried marijuana.

Marijuana possession is illegal in the state of California and it was not until 1996 when California voters approved Proposition 215 or Senate bill 420 that allows marijuana to be used for medical purposes only. The law required a medical doctor's recommendation for marijuana to be used for medical treatment.

I stepped out of the car and I held up the plastic baggie containing suspected marijuana. I asked Phil, Josh, Marshall and Tate, "Who is responsible for this bag of marijuana I just found?" Marshall said, "That's my weed". I placed Marshall under arrest for Health and Safety Code 11357(d) marijuana possession.

I placed Clay under arrest for driving on a suspended drivers license and forviolating California Vehicle Code 31, lying to the police as he told me he had a valid drivers license.

The emergency dispatcher informed me that the Josh's probation officer wanted him to be taken into custody as he had failed to meet with his court appointed probation officer and was to provide his probation officer with a current urine sample since he had "forgotten" to meet with his probation officer over a month ago.

Deputy Cramer transported Marshall and Josh to jail and I ordered a tow truck to tow and store Clay's car.

Passengers Tate and Phil were not wanted and they were allowed to leave. I saw them walk and stop about two blocks from where we were waiting for the tow truck and I bet their conversation was about me.

I requested a tow truck to remove Clay's car from the street. Another CVC 22651(h) towing authority. About ten minutes later the tow truck left with Clays' car and I drove towards Tate and Phil.

As my patrol car drew closer to them I saw they had a scared look on their faces and I responded by giving them a smirk. I was having another good day.

Day Three-Wednesday: Like the two days before I'm back in my spot at the convenience store parked under the cool tree reading current California criminal codes. And like the two days prior I noticed four cars pull up to the front of the convenience store.

I watched as about fourteen non-students took their position on the sidewalk. A couple of them look at me and all I did was smirk at them. (gobble gobble)

For some unknown reason the non-students were very quiet and I did not hear any smart "Kindergarten cop "remarks coming from their sidewalk positions.

The lunch bell rang and like before students from the high school were going in and out of the convenience store with their junk food lunch.

Like before I made the announcement that lunch was about to end in ten minutes. The students began to head back to campus. The non-students just stood there hoping I would leave. I did not want to leave right now.

Suddenly the non-students quickly returned to their cars and at the same time they began to back up. For a minute it looked like a destruction derby contest as two cars almost collided with each other. I'm guessing they did not want to be the last car to leave the parking lot.

The cars left the parking lot one at a time and now I decided to travel in their direction. When the last car entered the public street I was directly behind it.

I was very impressed because the driver was not speeding but I could see the driver appeared to be watching me in his rear view mirror.

That's when it happened. The driver did not see three student pedestrians in the marked crosswalk. I witnessed the driver fail to yield to pedestrians in a marked crosswalk. That is a flagrant violation of California Vehicle Code 21950(a) and a citable offense.

I activated my red and blue emergency lights followed by a short blast of the siren and pulled the violator over.

I approached the driver and he said, "Yes, I know I didn't stop for the pedestrians but, I did not see them at the time". I responded with "Well today I'll give you a citation to remind you to always watch for pedestrians in a marked crosswalk".

I requested the driver to hand me his valid driver's license, his car registration and his current proof of auto insurance. The driver identified himself as Jason. The front seat passenger identified himself as Harvey with rear seat passengers as Tommy and Frank.

As before I had emergency dispatcher conduct a computer check on Jason's car. The dispatcher advised me that Jason's car had not been registered in over a year.

I walked to the rear of Jason's car to see his license plate and I noticed a current license plate tab attached to the rear license plate.

State law makes it mandatory for all cars to be currently registered under California Vehicle Code section 4000(a)(1). If a car had not been currently registered in over one year and one day, the car could be towed and stored until all fees were paid to the state.

DMV records indicated Jason's car did not have current auto registration and that the car registration had not been paid in over one year and yet I was looking at a current license plate tab on the rear license plate.

I asked Jason to step out of the car and join me on the sidewalk. I told Jason that DMV computer records indicated his license plate tab was expired. I asked Jason "Did the DMV make a mistake?"

Jason said, "Oh yeah, my friend stole a license plate tab and I bought if off of him. I just need some additional time to get my car registered because I was having problems getting the car smog certified".

I responded asking Jason, "So you are telling me that you knowingly bought a stolen license plate tab and you knowingly placed a stolen license plate tab on your car's rear license plate?"

Jason answer was, "Well yeah, I just needed some additional time to get my car smog certified". I asked Jason if he was willing to give me a written statement about the license plate tab. Jason agreed and I took out a statement form. I requested back up and once again Deputy Cramer responded to my location.

I read Jason his Miranda rights and like he promised, he admitted to buying a stolen license plate tab and placing a stolen license plate tab on his car. (Jason was living proof that there was no lifeguard in his family gene pool)

Jason's statement was short and to the point. After he signed the written statement I informed Jason he was now under arrest for vehicle registration fraud.A misdemeanor crime under California Vehicle Code 4462.5.

I handcuffed Jason and placed him in the back of my patrol car. I informed passengers Harvey, Tommy and Frank that they were free to walk home because I was going to tow Jason's car.

They did not say anything to me they just quickly started

walking away from us. I would see them look over their shoulders every now and then but they walked like they had a very important appointment to make.

After the tow truck removed Jason's car, another CVC 22651(h) towing authority, I transported Jason to jail. (Jail is where we keep a lot of our stupid crooks that needs constant supervision). I was having a good day.

Day Four-Thursday: I took my usual spot again in my parking spot at the convenience store and once again I noticed the non-students entering the parking lot in their cars.

There were not so many old beat up cars as before and not so many non-students as before but they were there. I noticed their cocky swagger was gone and that they all had a nervous look on their faces but I was ready.

The students were on their lunch break and they were in and out of the convenience store for junk food lunches. I just sat in my patrol car watching everyone.

I made the ten minutes announcement and students waked back to campus. The non-students slowly returned to their cars and they slowly drove through the parking lot.

I decided to leave the convenience store parking lot at the same time. I was directly behind the last car leaving the lot. That's when I saw it.

The car I was behind was newer four-door model Ford Taurus sedan with a California exemption license plate attached to the rear bumper. Only government employees drove cars with California exemption license plates. The driver was about 19 years old non-student and he did not look like a government employee.

Once we were on the public street I activated my blue and red emergency lights followed by a short burst with the emergency siren. The car pulled over to the curb next to the high school student parking lot.

I approached the driver that identified himself as Travis. I asked Travis for his valid driver's license, his car registration and his current proof of auto insurance. Travis only had a driver's license.

I asked Travis if he was a government employee because he was operating a government owned vehicle. Travis informed me his mother worked with the county social services agency and the car was assigned to her.

I said, "Are you telling me your mother allowed you to drive this vehicle that is property of the county". Travis said, "Yeah, my mother said it was all right to drive her work car". I said, "Now we have a problem".

I asked Travis, "Right now where is your mother?" (This was before cell phones) Travis' reply to my question was "I don't know. My mother called in sick today and she is now at the shopping mall to do some shopping".

I informed Travis that his mother did not have the authority to allow him to use her assigned county work vehicle due to county policy and county insurance.

I asked emergency dispatchers to contact the county social services department and to notify the head administrator on duty. As we waited for a reply from the county administrators office Travis asked, "Can you not contact my mother's job because I don't want to get her in trouble".

I informed Travis it was too late because I could not legally allow him to drive a county owned vehicle. The responsibility against my department and me was far too great to allow that.

Again Travis asked, "Can you just follow me back home and I will just stay there and not say anything to anyone about this?" My answer was "No, so stop asking me for favors. I don't do favors for people that don't respect the law or respect the police".

As Travis and I stood on the sidewalk I noticed the front seat passenger was not wearing his seatbelt. The front seat passenger identified himself as Alex. I asked Alex why was he not wearing his seat belt. (Again with the seat belts?)

Alex snapped back at me and said, "I just took my seatbelt off!" I was happy to inform Alex that his seatbelt was caught in the car door and the seatbelt buckle was dragging on the ground. Alex opened the car door and saw the seatbelt was indeed caught in the door. His response was, "Oh".

I asked Alex for his ID because I was going to issue him a seatbelt citation. Alex asked, "Can you just give me a warning?" my answer was "No, not after you just lied to me about just taking off your seatbelt. Lying to the police is a bad habit".

Travis and I were still waiting for the social services administrator's call and I wrote out a citation to Alex for not wearing his seatbelt.

When I finished Alex's citation I started walking towards the car when the rear seat passenger Evan threw out an empty potato chip bag from the rear window. Wow, littering in front of a police officer. That is a flagrant violation of Penal Code 374.4.

I told Evan that I just witnessed him litter by throwing out that empty potato chip bag and I gave him a choice of getting out and finding the empty bag or get an expensive littering citation.

The other back seat passenger was Taylor and I heard him tell Evan, "Dude, just get out and get the bag because this psycho cop will give you a ticket." I took that comment as a compliment.

Alex signed his seatbelt ticket and Evan and Taylor began searching the school parking lot for that empty potato chip bag. They picked up more litter than they threw out and they walked over to a trashcan to throw it all away. What good eco-conscious citizens they were.

When they were done I heard Alex yell out, "We picked up all the litter. Can we go?" they were about twenty-five yards away and I answered them by just waving good-by to them. They were quick to leave and I saw them walk away in a hurry. I guess they had an important appointment to make, like the others.

Travis asked to leave and I said, "No, not now because I need answers as to why you were driving a county owned vehicle".

Travis then admitted he took his mother's assigned work car without her permission. I asked Travis if he was willing to give me a written statement about taking the car. Travis said "Yes, because I don't want to get my mother in trouble with her work".

I read Travis his Miranda rights and he and I stood on the sidewalk for a formal written statement. Travis admitted he took his mother's assigned county work vehicle after she called in sick at work that morning.

His mother left with a friend to go shopping at a local shopping mall. That's when he called his friends and they drove around town looking for girls and stuff. (Maybe doing illegal drugs to get high was their stuff)

As the lunch period began Travis drove to the convenience store to meet his other friends. Travis thought driving a newer looking car would prevent him from being stopped by law enforcement.

Travis ended by saying, "I've taken the county car a couple of times before and my mom caught me driving it, but this time I got caught by the police." I asked Travis, "You do realize you are confessing to embezzling a county owned vehicle?" Travis answered, "Yes, I just don't want my mom to get fired for allowing me to drive her assigned car". (My grandfather once told me if you hang around stupid people you tend to do stupid things because stupidity is contagious).

I informed Travis he was under arrest for violating California Vehicle Code section 10854 embezzling a government vehicle and I placed him in handcuffs. I asked emergency dispatchers to call the county garage and have a county tow truck take a county owned vehicle to the county garage for storage. I would have a to fill out another 22651(h) form.

I transported Travis to jail and as I was leaving the county jail, I was informed by emergency dispatchers, that Travis's mother Janice was at the police station demanding to see me right now.

When I arrived at the police station about twenty minutes later, I walked into the lobby at the police station. Janice and her friend appeared to be very angry and I introduced myself.

Janice said, "So, you're Officer Gill? The same officer that is harassing my son and his friends?"I informed Janice that if her adult son had a complaint he could contact my supervisor. I asked Janice if I could help her with something else.

Janice asked, "Where is my county vehicle right now?" (She did not ask about her son Travis, she just wanted information about her assigned county vehicle)

I informed Janice that Travis was driving around town in her assigned county vehicle and I stopped him near the high school after he and his friends were loitering around the convenience store.

I went on to say that I was unable to locate her after the traffic stop so I contacted her supervisor at the county administrators office. I saw the expression drop from Janice's face. I went on to inform her that the county tow truck took her assigned county vehicle to the county garage for storage.

For some unexplained reason her attitude took a complete change. I ended saying her county supervisor wanted a copy of my police report as he was going to conduct an internal investigation on the incident.

Janice and her friend began to slowly walk towards the front door of the police station. That's when I noticed her shopping bag was left behind.

I said, "Excuse me! But your Macy's shopping bag is here and it looks like it is full of expensive medicine to help you recover from your sick day".

Janice returned to take her shopping bag and she left the police station without saying a word. I think she had to go home

51

and come up with a good plan for work.

It was another good day for me.

Day Five-Friday: Like all the earlier days that week I was again in my space at the convenience store when I heard a car approaching. I heard it because the car radio was extremely loud.

Two cars turned into the convenience store parking lot and like in a movie all the drivers and passengers looked at my car parked under the cool tree. Suddenly their loud car radios went off immediately. I was waiting and watching for the cars to park in front of the convenience store but I was surprised to see the cars continue to drive slowly through the parking lot without stopping.

I just then decided to drive in their direction. The two cars entered the main roadway and I drove behind them. Again I was surprised to see the two drivers were doing a good job of maintaining good driving habits.

They were not speeding and they used their turn signal. Both drivers had their hands on the steeringwheel. All passengers appeared to be staring straight ahead and there was no talking to distract the driver. It was like watching Driver's ED 101. I was impressed.

We drove in the same direction for about seven blocks when I decided to make a right turn on a main street and return to the convenience store.

When I made it back to the store a large group of students were having lunch on the sidewalk and in the empty parking lot. It was a good sight to see because all the non-students had something else better to do that day. (Maybe they had important appointments with judges, lawyers, long DMV lines and tow truck companies)

I backed into my parking space at the convenience store and I decided to make an important announcement to all the students. I walked to the sidewalk in front of the store and I noticed a lot of students parted ways as I approached them.

It was time to make my announcement to the students. I started by saying in a loud tone, "Attention students. I have an announcement to make so all of you gather around to hear it". When they slowly gathered around me I said," Look at the trash can to my left".

I walked about five or six steps to my left and I pointed to an empty trash can. I said, "This TRASH CAN! is empty and I look around this parking lot and I see lot's of trash on the GROUND! As of today, if I see any student throwing trash on the ground I will issue that student a very expensive littering ticket! That means you and one of your parents will have to go to court to pay that expensive ticket. It would be a good gesture on your part to clean up the parking lot and put your trash in this empty TRASH CAN!! I will be right back with my citation book." I walked towards my patrol car and like before the students parted so that I could pass.

When I reached my patrol car I was surprised to see about thirty students picking up trash and placing their trash in the empty trash can. It was a good sight to see that the students were suddenly very interested and concerned about the environment.

I watched them for about five minutes and when it was time I made the usual announcement that lunch period was over in about ten minutes. Students quickly left the convenience store parking lot and they quickly headed back to class.

I walked inside the convenience store and the manager began to thank me. I must have heard thank you about three dozen times. I repeated you're welcome over and over. I walked to the rear of the store and I took out a bottle of water from the large wall cooler.

I returned to the counter and the store manager refused to take my money. He said, "You got rid of all those very bad men that used to come to my store. Thank you Officer, Thank you".

I handed the store manager my business card and I told him,

"I was assigned to the school district and if he was having troubles with any of the students just call the number and together we could work on solving the problem."I also suggested he contact the landlord and place signs on the building informing non-customers that it was illegal to loiter or trespass on the property under California Penal Code section 602.1

I left money on the counter and I walked out the front door. Again, I heard a lot of "thank you's".

When I stood on the sidewalk outside the convenience store I took a look at the parking lot. I said to myself the students did a great job of cleaning this parking lot. I guess they were motivated to do a good job. I walked over to the trash can and saw it was full of trash.

As I stood on the sidewalk outside the convenience store admiring the clean up work the owner of the beauty salon next to the convenience store approached me.

She said, "Thank you for all your hard work to change things for the better."

I replied, "You are welcome."

She went on to say, "For weeks business has been real bad because my customers, many of them senior citizens, did not want to deal with rude, obnoxious kids and a bunch of stoners and hoodlums (her words) hanging around the convenience store during lunch time".

I handed her my business card and told her that I was assigned to the school district. I informed her to call the number if there was a problem and together we can work to solve the problem.

I placed my empty water bottle in the near full trash can and I drove around the campus on my regular patrol. It was a good turkey hunt week.

When it was over I arrested seven subjects, wrote fifteen citations, towed four cars and made a lot of adult non-students (aka turkeys) nervous and unwelcome in the area. In my opinion they were all good examples of why not to use drugs because their brains were probably burned out due to all their substance abuse.

I made the owners and managers of the strip mall very happy, the court system happy and tow truck drivers very happy. I was having a good week.

My beat around the high school and the convenience store next to the school was very quiet but other police beats suddenly had a surge in crime.

I learned later that two of the subjects that used to loiter around the convenience store were arrested after a high-speed police pursuit in a stolen car. Three other subjects were arrested in a daytime home burglary. Two subjects were persons of interest in a drug related shooting and one subject was arrested and later convicted of rape of a sixteen-year-old girl in a local park. My police officer's hunch about a bunch of adult non-students loitering around high school students during their lunch period was correct.

Another problem solved by the SRO and community policing at work.

Chapter Five

A JUVENILE SPIDER MAN

On a Monday morning I received a call from Assistant Principal Jim Freeman at Fallon Middle School regarding a theft of school property. Mr. Freeman said, "Someone broke into the school over the weekend and stole three lap top computers and a video camera."

Freeman went on to say the school made a special announcement after the morning national anthem and offered a reward for information. Later two students who wanted to remain anonymous, told Mr. Freeman that 8th grader David broke into the school and stole school property.

Mr. Freeman told me that David would be a hard case and that he would never admit to the theft. I said, "Let's see, call him in for an interview." Mr. Freeman called David out of class and the interview began.

David said with a cocky attitude, "You don't have anything against me, so go for it." I told Mr. Freeman that I was taking David to the police station and that I would contact his mother when we arrived at the station. David still had the cocky attitude as I placed him un-handcuffed in my patrol car.

I had David wait for his mother in a separate office, with a snack and a soft drink, while I typed myself a letter on official police letterhead. The letter looked legitimate. (The law allows police to trick suspects)

The letter was from Dr. Gil Grissom with the CSI crime lab.

The television series CSI was a popular show and many kids believed DNA was easy to obtain with a super crime lab computer.

The letter read, "To Officer Gill from CSI crime scene technician Dr. Gil Grissom. This letter is to confirm David's DNA was recovered from the Fallon Middle School burglary. If needed, a letter could be sent to juvenile court to confirm our results and confirm a conviction against David for theft." I placed the CSI letter in a used envelope to convince David that I just received the evidence against him.

I allowed David to read the letter followed by me saying, "I'm getting a search warrant to search your room for the stolen computers and video camera. I will even find that dirty magazine hidden under your mattress." (I may have used this line before with another hard to confess student at another school)

David looked at me with a nervous look and said, "OK we stole the lap tops and video camera and yes it's in my room." I asked David, "Who is we?"

David said his friends Matt and Zach were with him.

I called Mr. Freeman and told him to call Matt and Zach out of class as David just confessed to breaking into the school and stealing the laptops and video camera. I told him I was on my way back to collect Matt and Zach. Mr. Freeman was surprised that I was able to get a confession from David.

When David's mother arrived I escorted them to a private office and I told her David and his two friends broke into the school over the weekend and they stole three lap top computers and a video camera. I told her some of the stolen property was in David's room and that I would transport David back to school for a special conference to discuss his possible suspension.

I requested that she return the stolen school property in David's room then she could meet with Mr. Freeman and myself at the school.

She located the stolen property and placed the stolen property on Mr. Freeman's desk. Mr. Freeman was shocked and surprised to see I solved the case with David's confession. David wrote a detailed confession on how the three were able to break into the school.

The three boys climbed on top of a lower classroom building and from there they used a maintenance ladder to gain access to the roof. Once the boys were on the roof they broke a plastic sky light cover and they used a rope that they brought to lower themselves to the classroom floor.

They placed the stolen property into backpacks they also brought with them and they simply walked out the front floor. The alarm did not sound until after they left the school building. The boys walked back to David's house with the stolen property in their backpacks. The police did respond to an alarm from the school but the officers left after all doors and windows were secure.

Matt and Zach were easy to confess once they learned that David told all about the theft. They added that all the planning was David's idea. All the boys were suspended from school because their plan was well thought out in advance and carried out like a military operation. I referred all three boys to juvenile court due to their advance planning in carrying out this crime.

Juvenile youth court is set up for juveniles to judge other juveniles accused of crimes. Some kids call juvenile youth court Peer Court because the prosecutor, defense counsel and even the jury are all kids like themselves. Superior court judges volunteer their time to listen to each case and juveniles volunteer as a prosecutor and defense attorney. The offending juvenile has to admit their crime in open court and the jury are all juveniles that were found guilty of their crimes on an earlier date.

The juvenile youth court jury are usually very tough on the juvenile offender and sanctions include several hours in community service, writing a letter of apology to the victim, hours of family counseling and serving as a juror for the next juvenile accused of committing a crime. Nothing like a little peer pressure.

Mr. Freeman wanted to know how I was able to obtain a confession and my reply was I had a little help from a super-fast pretend crime lab and the CBS televisions show CSI.

Another juvenile case solved by the SRO.

Chapter 6

GIVE ME SHELTER

It was a typical day at Castro Valley High School when the emergency dispatcher put out a call that a mother was trying to get her adult son named George help for his mental illness. The 70-year old mother wanted her 37-year-old son to take his prescribed medication. George was on state disability after he was diagnosed as a paranoid schizophrenic. George was under a doctor's care but he had refused to take his prescribed medication for about two days.

The fire department and an ambulance crew responded to that call for assistance. A couple of minutes later the fire captain requested police assistance because George was in the kitchen and he had armed himself with a large kitchen knife.

Two deputies answered the call and responded to assist the fire crew on scene. When the two deputies arrived they requested a deputy with a Taser gun to respond. (When this incident occurred in 1993, Tasers were issued only to a few deputies that went through the special training. It was not until 2001 that all deputies were issued Tasers after training). A deputy on the east end of town answered the assistance call and was on his way to join the deputies and fire crew.

Before the deputy with the Taser arrived, one deputy put out an emergency call announcing, "We got a runner!! He just turned rabbit on us!" meaning George was on the run. He left the house through the rear kitchen door and was now in the back yard. The two deputies gave chase but now George was over the back fence and was running towards the high school. Hey, that's my beat.

I drove towards the problem house because George's house was only a few blocks from the high school. I did not want any students from the high school to wander in the area while George was on the run with a large kitchen knife.

I pulled over to the side of the road near some adjacent houses so that students leaving the high school would see my patrol car and just turn around and go back to the high school.

It did not take long but I saw a man run out of an alley wearing no shoes and only his pajamas. The man stood about 6'4" and he weighed about 240 pounds. I said to myself, "I think that huge angry looking man is psycho George."

I saw the man duck behind a car parked on the street. I was thinking to myself, "What do I do? I really don't want to fight this huge guy."

I saw the man quickly stand up and run across the street and hide behind a garbage can. It was garbage collection day. Again I was thinking, "What am I going to do when George gets closer?"

I could hear police sirens from additional patrol cars on adjacent streets. Those patrol cars were from responding deputies to help search for George. It was too late. George approached me.

I decided to get out of the patrol car in case I had to get physical with him. I did not know what would happen to me if George decided to get violent.

As George drew closer I had to think of a quick plan. I asked George, "Are they chasing you?" and he replied "Yeah!" I then told George to "Quick, hide in the back seat of this car." I quickly opened the back door to my patrol car.

George did what I asked him to do and he simply got into my marked patrol car without a problem. It was strange but that was easy and it worked. I quickly closed the car door before George realized he was sitting inside a police car.

Wow, George was lying on the floorboard of my patrol car and he was hiding from other deputies that were searching for him.

I stood outside my patrol car and saw a couple of deputies quickly drive past me. They looked at me with a curious look on their faces. I just waved at them with a smirk on my face. They were probably wondering what I was doing, just standing there while a paranoid schizophrenic patient was running around.

I thought it was a little funny that George was hiding inside my patrol car. A couple of minutes went by and I saw another deputy drive by and he too had a curious look on his face as well. I was leaning against the side of my patrol car and I just waved at him.

It was funny, so to keep George in his position I would knock on the window and yell out "Stay down George because they are still looking for you." George kept his hands over his head and he remained in that position in the back seat and floorboard area.

Finally, a deputy slowed down and rolled down his patrol car's window and asked, "What are you doing Gill, we're looking for a runner."

I told him "You mean George? He's in the back seat of my car." The deputy asked, "George is in your car? How did you get him inside your car?" I answered with "that's not the problem, getting him out of the car will be the problem."

Soon four other deputies in patrol cars arrived and they were all looking at George lying on the floorboard of my patrol car. They all wanted to know how I did it. I just said, "I calmly asked George to hide inside my patrol car and he just got in."

The patrol sergeant arrived and the decision was made for me to drive George directly to John George Psychiatric Hospital. The sergeant was going to meet with the fire and ambulance crews still waiting at the house and have George's mother meet with his doctor at the mental health hospital.

Two deputies followed me to the hospital in case George decided to escape again. After driving a couple of miles with George in the back of the car, he sat up in the back seat.

I could see George from the rear view mirror and he asked me, "Where are we going?" I answered George saying, "We are going to meet your mother at the hospital."

I calmly asked George, "Why don't you like taking your medication?" George replied with, "The government is trying to brainwash me with pills" and "They are always spying on me and they are trying to control me with pills."

I said, "Wait a minute, that sounds like the old pills, the new pills will help you think better, like a NASA scientist or something."

George said, "I could work for NASA, so maybe I'll take the new pills."

I calmly told George to put his seatbelt on and George simply said, "Oh, OK". That was easy too. When I arrived at the John George Psychiatric Hospital two deputies assigned to the hospital were waiting for me.

I opened the back door to my patrol car and I calmly told George that his mother was on her way to the hospital and that she wanted him to wait for her inside the building with your doctor. Without a problem George said, "Oh, OK".

Two nurses arrived with a gurney and I told George to just get on the gurney so that the nurses could take care of him until his mother arrived. George was strapped down with five points restraints on the gurney without a problem and taken into the hospital.

It turned out to be a good day for the fire crews, the ambulance crew, the mental health doctors and nurses, the deputies and maybe even for NASA.

Another case solved by the SRO.

Chapter Seven

THE CARJACKING

I received an urgent call from Castro Valley High School campus supervisor Joyce regarding an attempted carjacking in the student parking lot off Mabel Avenue. That end of the high school campus is not very busy during the school day.

I met with Joyce and student Tommy in the student parking lot. Tommy told me that he was returning to school after a dental appointment and he was looking for a parking space when three non-students approached him.

The non-students wanted his car and they brandished a locking blade pocket knife during their demands. They forced him out of his car and they tried to drive off in his car. Tommy ran to the campus for help and he met with campus supervisor Joyce who was walking in the area.

The car they tried to steal was Tommy's grandfather's 1952 Rambler sedan with a standard transmission on the steering column. This type of transmission is called a "three on a tree" gearshift. That was a very old-school type of car.

One suspect was unable to get the car into gear and it rolled back and struck a parked car behind it. The car then stalled and the three juvenile suspects panicked and left the campus running towards the center of town.

Joyce told me that about a half-an hour earlier she encountered the three non-students on campus wanting to visit a girl in the 9th grade.

They did locate the girl they were looking for and they gave her a happy birthday balloon, some flowers and a birthday card. Joyce sent the girl back to class and told the three non-students to leave the campus. Joyce last saw them walking towards the student parking lot on Mabel street.

Joyce left me to go get the birthday girl out of class because the birthday girl would be able to identify the boys. Joyce returned to the student parking lot with our birthday girl Monica.

I asked Monica about the three boys that were on campus to visit her. She responded with a "I don't know them. You're the police, you find out who they are."

I responded saying, "This is a small town and I'm going to catch them walking down the street then I'm going to take them straight to juvenile hall. Once they are locked away, I'm coming back here to take you to juvenile hall on your birthday because you are lying to the police and you are obstructing a felony carjacking investigation."

Monica quickly thought about her situation and she told me in a tearful voice that they were all from Skyline High School in Oakland and that their names were Jamal, Wallace and Jovan. I told her that I would talk to her later because I had to go and arrest Jamal, Wallace and Jovan.

I drove towards the center of town and towards a main street bus stop. As I drove towards the bus stop I saw my suspects. The three were high school aged males and I did not recognize them as Castro Valley High School students. I rolled down the patrol car window and said, "Hello Jamal, Wallace and Jovan, why are you kids illegally cutting school today?"

They had a surprised look on their faces because I knew their names. They began looking at each other and they just stood frozen on the sidewalk. Finally, Jamal asked, "How do you know our names?" and I replied, "I'm the police, I know everything." I exited my patrol car and opened the back door to the passenger compartment to the patrol car.

I said, "You three were on the campus at Castro Valley High School and I'm taking you to the police station." I informed them that I know a knife was used and to hand over the knife. Jamal reached into his front pocket and handed me a large pocket knife. I told them to get into the back seat so they could go to the police station. They did what I instructed them to do without a problem.

I told them that Castro Valley High School staff and students identified them and that I was prepared to charge them with-felony-attempted car-jacking and brandishing a weapon (knife), in addition to trespassing on another school campus and causing a major disruption to a school.

I read the three their Miranda rights and Jamal confessed he forced the student out of his car and the other two suspects admitted they tried to steal the car to go home. After collecting their written statements, I called their parents. Two of the parents refused to come to the police station to pick-up their sons so I transported all three to juvenile hall.

After I was done booking my three carjackers, I returned to the high school to speak with the birthday girl Monica. She had a complete change in her attitude and she apologized for her behavior in the student parking lot. Monica attended school with all three suspects in the previous year and she did not want the reputation as being a "narc or a snitch".

I told Monica that a lot of cities have a serious crime problem because of the misguided "no snitch" beliefs. I added, "You should help your community and make it safe by telling what you know and you are not a snitch when you do the right thing."

I contacted Monica's parents by telephone and I told them she was involved but she helped with an incident that occurred at school. I referred her to a school counselor to work on a better attitude.

Another crime solved by the SRO.

Chapter Eight

CYBERBULLY COWARDS

Dublin High School teacher Brenda West was investigating a potential problem she was trying to prevent in her classroom.

Brenda told me she was investigating a case of suspected cyberbullying between five of her female students. I was told 10th grade student Heather was having problems with 10th grade students Rebecca, Alyson, Molly and Abby. Rebecca and Abby were at home and not on campus and Brenda told me she needed to speak with them to collect information in her cyberbullying investigation.

On Monday around 0800 hours I met with Brenda again to assist her with her concerns about suspected cyberbullying between the five female students.

Brenda told me she received a copy of Heather's Facebook posting and she suspected Rebecca was the author as Heather has great spelling and grammar and Rebecca had similar spelling and grammar that matched her printed copy of the Facebook post. Brenda also suspected Alyson, Molly and Abby were involved, as all three girls were close friends of Rebecca.

Brenda noticed that Rebecca had total control of her friends and that Rebecca's friends did whatever Rebecca wanted them to do. Brenda said, "Rebecca was the Queen Bee".

I asked Brenda if the girls were on campus and she replied Rebecca and Abby were not but they could be called back to campus. Brenda stated that as of an hour ago Heather's mother was on campus to address the threats made against her daughter Heather by the other four girls.

Heidi, Heather's mother, was on campus to complain to the assistant principal and address the cyberbullying threats made against her daughter Heather. Heidi gave me copies of a Facebook computer printout showing entries made on her daughter's Facebook page. Heidi stated she contacted Rebecca's mother by telephone and she informed Rebecca's mother of her suspicions.

As Brenda and I read the printouts given to me by Heidi, she received a cell phone call from Rebecca's mother Audrey. Heidi informed us that Rebecca just confessed to her mother that she sent Heather the threats on Heather's Facebook page.

Rebecca was able to get Heather's computer password and Rebecca admitted that she sent the cyberbullying message to get back at Heather. Rebecca also admitted to her mother that she had her friends Alyson, Molly and Abby send threatening messages to Heather's Facebook page as well.

Brenda called parents Audrey, the mother of Rebecca; Bridget the mother of Molly; Pam the mother of Abby; and Gina mother of Alyson. I asked them to escort their daughters to school so that we could speak with them about the computer threats.

Brenda informed Assistant Principal Madelyn Barns, that students Rebecca, Alyson, Molly and Abby admitted they sent the harassing and threatening computer messages to Heather by way of Facebook. Barns arranged for a special conference with the parents and girls for that afternoon.

Around 1300 hours, teacher Brenda West, Assistant Principal Madelyn Barns, all the parents and students involved met in the administrator's conference room to discuss the cyberbullying message.

We learned that Rebecca and Heather have been disagreeing with each other since the 5th grade. We discussed some of the reasons why students cyberbully each other on line. The girls and parents listened to Assistant Principal Barns and dialogs from the parents but I was not happy with the special conference.

I listened to the girls and my impression of them was too much reality television. Now I'm looking at a group of mean girls that are spoiled brats and now they think they are entitled to behave anyway they want.

I'm an old Marine platoon sergeant and I could see Rebecca's (Queen Bee) face and she appeared bored and she just wanted to leave. I felt all the girls were not taking the special conference as a serious response to their behavior. I decided to speak up and I do not hold back or sugar coat my message. I was about to open a can of worms but I felt I had to speak up.

I started off saying, "I noticed Rebecca, Alyson, Molly and Abby were not listening to any of the adults because I saw them looking at each other and smiling, just looking at the celling or just staring off hoping that everyone would just shut up so they could just leave because they are just bored. Because of their expressions, I'm under the impression that they are not taking the cyberbullying threats very seriously."

Immediately the girls began to object about my statements and about my observations of them. The mothers began to make excuses for their daughter's behaviors and I continued to speak my mind.

I said, "The Internet provides the perfect forum for cyberbullies and the Internet gives the narcissistic bullya sense of satisfaction by sending people they don't like flame mail and hate mail while they can remain completely anonymous like a cyber coward.

Their computer keyboard aggression and false criticism help the cyberbully create conflict and they gain needed attention. The cyberbully gains power, control, domination and their friends go along with the harassment to avoid becoming cyberbullied themselves."

As before the mother's began to defend their daughters and they claimed they always monitored their daughters all the time.

I asked the mothers if they monitored their daughter's computers, were they also monitoring their daughter's cell phones. Their reply was "Yes, of course we do". I said, "So you're all too familiar with the latest cell phone acronyms that kids use on their cell phone to keep their parents clueless."

Suddenly Rebecca, Alyson and, Abby and Molly began to look at each other with a nervous look on their faces. (I think I have the girl's attention now). I went on to ask the mothers if they knew the latest Internet texting slang and not just LOL for laugh out loud.

Now that I have everyone's complete attention. I informed the mothers that kids today are very tech savvy and they had their own type of shorthand for their cell phones.

Now the room was completely quiet and again Rebecca, Alyson, Molly and Abby had a nervous look on their faces because I was about to reveal a possible secret they had been keeping from their mothers.

I said, "Moms take out your pens and paper because I'm going to give you top secret CIA codes kids use on their cell phones to keep their parents completely clueless about what they are texting their friends".

I said, "Collect your daughter's cell phones and follow my instructions, I'll help you crack the secret code" the moms asked their daughters for their cell phones and after a short argument with them all the cell phones were collected.

I started with first lesson. Acronyms like LMK- Let me know and WYCM – Will you call me is innocent but look for GNOC- Get naked on camera, IWSN – I want sex now, NIFC – Naked in front of computer, 420- Marijuana, POS-Parent over shoulder, LC6- Lets have sex and KPC- Keep parents clueless.

Parent Audrey asked how could they learn all the acronyms their kids use and I said, "Just Google them like I did and you will get a complete list of all the acronyms used on your daughter's cell phones".

The daughters began to protest what I was telling their moms saying things like, "that is some kids but not us", and "we don't do that". I told the moms that I once had a teenage son and whenever I heard him say "that's other kids, that's not me" or "I don't do that," that it usually is a secret kid's code meaning,"I'm lying to you because I do it too so, please don't check". Another tipoff is when my son would say, "Don't you trust me" which is code for "I'm gambling and hoping you will just drop the topic and don't check." My response to him was "Yes, I trust you but I don't know your friends and I don't trust them." Some kids do not feel guilt when they lie to their parents about what they are really doing.

Parent Bridget said, "I can't find any messages on my daughter's cell phone" and I said, "Kids hide their text messages with decoy apps." Now the girls were really nervous and they took a very deep breath hoping I would just stop talking to their moms.

I said, "Decoy apps may look like a calculator or a music app to throw off suspicious parents." The decoy apps will hide text messages and pictures on their cell phone. "If the calculator needing a password that may not be a calculator, it could be a decoy app." Now I was watching moms closely looking at their daughter's cell phones. I went on and told the moms that kids give their parents a password to their cellphones but the decoy app will have a separate password to secure it from their parents.

Parent Bridget asked how do you know all this stuff and I again said, "Just Google your question like I did and you can get answers."

Parent Gina said her daughter's app needed a password but Alyson would not give her mom her cell phone password. Mrs. Barns suggested she could contact the school district's IT department and maybe they could have a computer specialist come over and break the code to obtain her password. Again I heard a lot of crying from the girls. Alyson decided to begrudgingly cooperate and she gave her mother her secret password.

Next, I tried to explain how kids jail break their cell phones where they can disable their cell phones with an app that will completely take the app off of their cell phones screen. Later when needed all they have to do is touch a blank part of their screen and the special app is activated again.

Suddenly parent Audrey discovered her daughter's secret app with two large file folders. When Audrey opened one file she was shocked to find her daughter had nude photos of her in the file. In the other file were copies of several cyberbully messages sent to other girls attending school. Now we may have several other possible victims.

When I heard Audrey say Rebecca had nude photos on her cell phone I said, "Because of Rebecca's nude photos on her cell phone we have a new problem so let's talk about cyberbullying later."

I explained to the moms and girls that the nude photos on their cell phone may be a violation of California Penal Code 311- (Child Pornography Law).

I told them that the way I understood the law if nude photos were taken of any child under 18 years of age it may be considered child pornography. If the nude photos were sent to another person that act may be considered distribution of child pornography and if the person accepting the nude photos is 18 years old or older that person can be charged with felony possession of child pornography. If the adult is convicted of possession of child pornography, he or she may be required to register as a sex offender under California Penal Code 290.

Rebecca the Queen Bee began to cry and now Rebecca's friends began to cry as well because they knew it was only a matter of time before their moms discovered their secret apps and folders.

This can of worms I just opened was now becoming out of control. The room was full of crying girls, angry mothers and shocked school officials. I needed to take control again.

I began by saying, "Let's all take a look at the big picture here. A lot of trust was broken but we can learn from what we just discovered. Moms, let's work on a strategy to educate your daughters, it's not too late".

I began with the girls explaining that, "Some social sites can be dangerous. You should always keep your personal information private. Just because you deleted some information on your computer or cell phone that does not mean it is gone forever. The information you deleted can still be retrieved."I said, "Girls, always think before you share."

Next I spoke with the mothers. I said, "Moms, now is the time to discuss how social media can impact your daughters lives because the girls have to realize that colleges and future employers are going to be looking at their social media activity."I went on to explain how inappropriate comments and photos can come back to haunt them years later because once something is shared on the Internet it will remain in cyberspace for eternity but curious people may be able to access it and look at their past at any time.

Since I now had the girl's attention I asked them, "Years from now when you are a mom, how would you feel if your own children located an old photo of you in your birthday suit from your old high school days. Would you like them to see your old nude photos being passed around by your children?" They all said "No."

I told them, "Well that is how your moms are feeling right now," and "Private things between family members should remain private."

Suddenly I had moms and daughters crying again. How can I stop this and get everyone back? (I thought to myself that I should have bought stock in Kleenex!)

I told the girls, "Today your mothers discovered you broke their trust, and their hearts, but you can earn their trust back. It will take a lot of work on your part but you can earn their trust again. It will just take time for things to heal and to get better but you have to change to make things better. Your mothers gave you life and they have thought of nothing but good for each of you from that day on. Your mothers have always been on your side."

Next I said, "Moms today you learned the hard way that your daughters made a mistake but it could have been worse if they were physically hurt because of their mistakes. There are people out there looking for kids that keep secrets from their parents. We all make mistakes and now you know what to focus on and how to help your daughters. We all learned something today so let's focus on really talking about a lot of important issues; and girls,you need to work with your mothers because someone will have to explain everything to your dads." I saw what appeared to be a collective "Oh no, what are we going to tell dad?!" look on everyone's face. (Attention all boys, be on the lookout for a group of real angry dads).

I explained California Penal Code 528.5PC (California cyber-bulling law which took effect on New Years Eve 2011) to Rebecca, Allyson, Molly and Abby.

Rebecca (aka Queen Bee) reached out and began hugging and crying in her mom's arms. Rebecca said, "I love you mom. I'm so sorry." It didn't take long but all the girls began hugging and crying with their moms. (I said to myself, I'm finally back in control and I really should have bought stock in tissue).

Brenda stated she would assign the girls to different areas and desks to avoid problems in class and Brenda also stated she and her classroom assistant would monitor Rebecca and Heather closer in the future.

Assistant Principal Barns assigned an in-house suspension to all the girls with restrictions to stay off the computer.

All the parents stated they would take away all of their daughter's cell phone and home computer privileges to prevent another Facebook harassment complaint and to really talk with their daughters about Internet safety. I suggested each mom should Google their questions about the dangers of the Internet.

The school administrator and teacher told me that the special conference, in their opinion ended well, with mothers and daughters leaving school with a lot of important personal issues to discuss.

Assistant Principal Barns and teacher Brenda contacted parent Heidi by telephone and they gave Heidi the outcome of the special conference.

Another case solved by a good teacher, a good school administrator and supportive parents helping their SRO.

Chapter Nine

THE COMPUTER HACKER

I received a call from Assistant Principal Terry Young at Dublin High School regarding a case of computer hacking that she was investigating.

Mrs. Young told me the case came to her attention through school counselor Mrs. Carol Roberts. Mrs. Roberts met with a parent that wanted to thank her for helping her son Jason get better grades and improve his school attendance. The problem was Mrs. Roberts did not work with her son and had no idea what the parent was talking about.

Mrs. Young and Mrs. Roberts took a look at 10th grader Jason's grades and school attendance and saw that his attendance was perfect and his grades jumped from C-and D's to all A's and B+. They called Jason's teachers and learned that Jason did not attend class at all and his grades were predicted to be even lower than recorded. (Houston, we have a problem)

The school district had their computer technicians come to the high school to locate the computer Jason used to hack into the school's main computer.

The school districts computer specialist was able to locate a possible computer that Jason used. The computer used was in the attendance office. Mrs. Young recalled for a short time Jason worked as a student assistant in the attendance office.

The technician also spotted other juveniles had suspicious changes on their school grades and school attendance records.

The technician gave the names of four students with suspicious activities on their school account.

I asked Mrs. Young if the students on the list were friends of Jason. The names were Paula, Vera, Steve and Brian. Mrs. Young immediately recognized Steve and Brian as Jason's friends but not the girls. Mrs. Young called Steve and Brian's teacher and learned their grades were changed as well as their school attendance.

Now we have additional suspects to interview. Maybe one will break under a little pressure during their interview with their assistant principal and their SRO. We only need one to talk. Mrs. Young felt Paula was the weak link needed to break the case.

Mrs. Young and I called Paula to the office and we interviewed her. I explained to Paula that we were investigating a breach of security to the school computer system. I asked her to explain the grades and school attendance changes on her school record. I also let her know that we spoke to all of her teachers and we obtained her current grades from her teacher's workbook. Paula immediately broke down and started to cry. Paula said, "I knew we would get caught. I don't know why I let Jason talk me into it."

When she was able to calm down she told us that Jason told her he was able to hack into the school's computer and that he was able to change his grades and school attendance. She continued, "Jason offered to change my grades and attendance for $50." Paula agreed to the grades and school attendance change so that she could go to school whenever she felt like attending class. Paula gave me a two-page written statement detailing how Jason hacked into the school's computer system while he temporarily worked as a student assistant in the attendance office. Now we had some evidence against Jason.

I called Vera into my office and she immediately cracked and told us the same story Paula told. Vera was easier than

Paula and she gave me a three-page written statement, again naming Jason as being responsible for hacking into the school's computer and changing her grades and school attendance. Additional evidence against Jason.

Now it was Steve's turn to confess and give a statement against Jason. Steve was a little harder to confess but after an hour of going back and forth with the truth he finally cracked and gave a two-page confession admitting paying $50 for a grade and school attendance change.

Now it was Brian's turn to interview about his part in the school computer hacking and grades and attendance changes. Brian gave a two-page confession accusing Jason of hacking into the school computer. Now I had four confessions against Jason.

With all the written confessions against Jason he saw that lying about his crime would not help and he admitted to hacking into the school computer. Jason offered to assist the school district with detailing huge holes in the computer security system so that other juveniles working as student assistants could not do the same computer crimes.

Mrs. Young told Jason that his school crime was taken as a very serious breach of school security and that the principal wanted him to go before the school superintendent for a review. Jason admitted he only made his confession so that he could stay in school.

We learned later after reviewing his school file that Jason attended another high school a year earlier. In the file Jason was suspected of committing the same type of security breach at his former high school. Jason was expelled because of that computer incident and now his current school district office wanted Jason to go before their school board in an expulsion hearing.

Jason was very advanced with covering his tracks to avoid being caught however Jason did not count on his customers wanting to stay out of trouble and simply staying in school. Jason was referred to juvenile youth court due to the repeat pattern of breaching school computer security.

Another crime solved by the Assistant Principal and the SRO.

Chapter Ten

THE SRO THAT RAPPED MUSIC

During my daily patrol around Castro Valley High School, I happened to notice three tenth grade boys hanging around the loading dock area of the school cafeteria during the school lunch period. They were not doing anything wrong but I found it very curious that they were always there and not eating lunch with the other students. We never spoke to each other we just gave each other the "look".

After seeing them in the same spot everyday for about two weeks just giving each other the look, I happened to see campus supervisor Joyce walking in the area. I asked Joyce who the three students were.

Joyce told me she called the three students the "rappers" and that they were all new students after being transferred from three other schools. Students told Joyce in confidence that the three would make threats and bully them with their words so all the other students tried to avoid contact with them.

One was named Marcus from Oakland, the other was named Manny from Hayward and the third was named Freddy from Fremont. Joyce ended telling me Marcus had a "chip on his shoulder" because she had to warn him a couple of times to not use profanity and stop threatening other students on campus.

A couple of days later I was sitting in my school campus office fighting boredom when I used the school district computer to look up the emergency card information on my three rappers.

I noticed Marcus lived in the same apartment complex that I once lived in when I first moved to the Bay Area in 1975. Marcus lived in the very same apartment I once had, what a coincidence. I did nothing with the information because they were not doing anything wrong other than possibly bullying or threatening other students at school.

Then one day at the end of school I was driving back to the police station when I noticed Marcus walking home. Marcus had detention that day and he was walking alone. It was beginning to rain so I pulled over to the side of the road and I rolled do the window to my patrol car to speak with Marcus.

I yelled out to him and offered him a ride home before he was soaking wet from the rain. I said to Marcus "Hey, do you want a ride home?" Marcus responded saying, "I don't want to ride home in a police car!" My response to that comment was "are you telling me you don't have enough sense to get out of the rain?" As Marcus stood there thinking about my comment the rain began to fall harder. I ended saying, "It's your decision but right now I'm dry sitting in my car, are you wet or dry?"

Marcus asked if he should "get in the back seat" and I told him to "get in the front seat because you are not in custody for anything, you're just wet." Marcus quickly sat in the front seat of the patrol car. I noticed he had a surprise look on his face and he said, "I've never sat in a police car before."

Marcus said he lived on Wilbeam Ave. and I told him that I know where he lived. "How do you know where I live," he asked and I responded telling him "I'm the police and I know everything." The wheels in his head must have been turning and wondering. I didn't tell him my little secret that many years ago I once lived in the exact same two-bedroom apartment that he and his mother now occupy.

I told him that kids at school call him and his friends the rappers. Why do they call you guys the rappers? Because, he answered, that is what I want to be in a couple of years from now.

I told him rap music was a hard business to get started in and he told me he knew what to do to get his name in the game.

I asked Marcus if his family knew about his plans and he answered telling me his father was in prison for murder, his older brother was killed selling drugs and his mother was too busy working to support him and her. Marcus told me he did not expect to live past 30 years but that was all part of the rap music game. All he wanted was gold jewelry, a BMW car and lots of girls hanging around him. According to Marcus that was his only future.

I dropped him off in front of his apartment and I started thinking about how to change Marcus's mind about his future. On the way home I stopped by a bookstore and I bought several books.

One book was on rap music. The book had the words used in rap music so I could understand what the rapper was saying. That was a big help for me. The other books were on people that succeeded in school and in life. They were also on sale.

I took the books to school and on Monday morning I saw Marcus and his friends in their usual hangout. I called Marcus over and I made him a bet.

The bet was that I could rap one of his songs and if I won he had to read a book. At first he did not want to make the bet but after challenging him that I could rap a song in just a week he agreed and the bet was made. I did not tell him that thanks to Barnes and Nobel I had a book on rap music. I guess that little bit of information just slipped my mind.

A week later I met with Marcus, Manny and Freddy and I rapped a song for them. The song I rapped was "Dangerous Minds" by rapper Coolio. Wow! The boys were shocked to hear an old deputy sheriff rapping one of their songs. I won the bet and I gave Marcus a book to read.

The book was a biography of four-star General Colin Powell.

I told Marcus that I would check with him next Monday after he read the book and I would rap another song once he read the biography.

The following Monday morning we met again and I rapped another song for them. The song was "La Raza" by Hispanic rapper Kid Frost. Wow! I did it again but now I rapped to them in Spanish. We discussed the General Colin Powel biography and they learned he was once an average student like them that grew up to be a great leader. General Colin Powel went through ROTC in college and served in Vietnam before being appointed as Chairman of the Joint Chief of Staff and advisor to the President of the United States.

Since I won the bet I gave Marcus his second book to read. The book was a biography on George Washington Carver. A week later we met again and I rapped a song by TLC called "Don't Go Chasing Waterfalls." All of a sudden they wanted to talk with me whenever I saw them during my daily patrol around the school.

We discussed the biography of George Washington Carver and they learned that he was a former slave that taught himself how to read and write and he became the leading authority and inventor of over 200 uses for the peanut. They were impressed.

I won another bet and I gave them the biography of Garret Morgan. As usual we met at their spot but now they did not want to hear a rap song. They wanted to discuss the biography of Garret Morgan.

The three boys were surprised to learn that an African-American who had a simple high school education and a lot of common sense invented the everyday traffic light.

I was slowly changing their minds and our meeting on Mondays became more about current events and people in the news rather than just rap music. I would always leave them saying, "You don't have to go to jail like a gangsta to be famous and we in law enforcement don't need their business so stay in school and be successful." I told them to study hard, go to college and become famous by doing something good that can help others. I would also tell them, "Let them write books about your success and not your arrest and failures."

The school went into winter break and I did not see the three boys for a while. When break was over I did not see them at their usual spot.

I learned from campus supervisor Joyce that the three boys were spending all their time in the school library during the lunch periods. What became of my future rappers? They are in the school library?

They kept a low profile on and off campus and I would see them in passing or walking home after school. A couple of times they flagged me down to get a ride home in my police car. That was a complete change in attitudes and I was happy to see that.

Then the next thing you know it was graduation time. I would always attend graduation and on Marcus's graduation day he was frantically looking for me. Marcus wanted me to meet his mother and he wanted to take a photo of the two of us with him in his graduation gown.

Marcus's mother, Rita, told me her son spoke of me often and she was proud of him as he was planning on going to college. Rita told me Marcus would be the first member in her family to attend college. It was a good graduation day for the both of them and for me.

Right after the graduation ceremonies I met the parents of Manny and Freddy as well. Manny was planning on attending college and Freddy planned on joining the military to see the world before committing to anything like getting married and starting a family. We all took many after graduation photos and I wished my rappers well. It was a good day for me.

It was several years later but I received a surprise visitor at the police station. It was the now adult Marcus and he wanted to share that he graduated from the University of Santa Cruz and he was planning on getting married. I learned that his friend Manny attended college and was the branch manager of a local bank. Freddy served in the military and was honorably discharged and was working as a paramedic and firefighter in the City of Hayward.

Marcus wanted to know if I was willing to write him a letter of referral, as he wanted to become an Oakland Police Officer. I told Marcus I would be happy to write a referral if he promised to help at least one kid to finish school and make a better life for himself. We shook hands and the deal was made.

Good job Marcus, Manny and Freddy.

Chapter Eleven

GANG COLORS THAT BLEED

It was the beginning of a new school year in Dublin and students and parents were enrolling in their new schools. Summer break was over and students went about their day at their new campuses. There was a lot of activities and meeting with their old school friends as well as meeting new school friends.

As I did many times before, I was sitting in my parked patrol car during the lunch period at the Valley Continuation High School when I met with another Deputy to discuss an important police matter. We were deciding where we were going to have lunch.

Deputy Ramos met with me in the staff parking lot and we sat in our patrol cars to talk. I sat in my patrol car facing north and Ramos approached my patrol car and he sat in his patrol car facing south.

As Ramos and I talked my cell phone rang. It was the continuation school secretary Bridget. Bridget said, "Officer Gill we just had a student stabbed on campus." I said, "Confirm a student was just stabbed on campus?" and she said, "Yes a student was just stabbed, do I call 911? We need you on campus, where are you right now?" I told Bridget that I was sitting in the campus parking lot and that I will be in the office in about 30 seconds.

I drove towards the continuation school main office and I informed 911 dispatchers that Officer Ramos and I were on the continuation school campus investigating a student that was just stabbed on campus. I requested an ambulance to respond to the school code three (Emergency response with lights and sirens).

I walked into the main office area of the continuation high school and I saw a student sitting in a chair as school secretary Robin was applying a bandage to a bleeding male juvenile. I saw the juvenile was bleeding from the stomach and chest area. Principal Marjory was on the telephone with the school superintendent's office.

I recommended the school go into lock-down due to the stabbing and Officer Ramos went out to his patrol car to get a first-aid kit and help Robin control the bleeding of the student in the main office.

I asked Bridget "Who stabbed the student and where is he now?"

Many students were in shock with a couple of female students in a corner crying. I overheard them say, "Kenny did it Officer Gill and Kenny is outside the building about to leave right now!"

I was very familiar with 17-year-old Kenny as he was just transferred to the continuation high school from Dublin High School due to his grades and attendance dropping for some unknown reason. I stepped outside the main office using the north door and immediately saw Kenny talking with three students.

Kenny had his back turned away from me and he did not see me quickly approaching him. I saw Kenny was handing things from his pockets to the student he was talking too. They saw me approaching and I yelled out "Give Kenny all his property back and get to class! The school is on lock down!" The students did what I said and they gave Kenny back all the items (also known as evidence) he was handing them. They quickly went into a classroom.

I approached Kenny and I said, "Turn around Kenny and cuff up" Kenny did as he was instructed and I placed Kenny in handcuffs. I searched Kenny and located a bloody 6-inch locking blade pocket knife in his right pants pocket.

I was surprised at Kenny's violent action on campus because we had a long understanding of each other. I had known Kenny since he was in the 5th grade and I knew his family history. Kenny lived with his widowed grandmother as his mother died of cancer when he was a small baby. Kenney's father was serving time in prison. Kenny's grandmother was very active with his school activities and she and I would cheer for Kenny when he played varsity football at the Dublin High School. I would even give Kenny a ride home after football practice on dark and rainy nights. Kenny was always polite and his grandmother worked hard to keep Kenny happy.

I said, "Kenny your grandmother is going to be crushed after she hears about what happened at school today."

Kenny answered saying "I know I let her and you down today Officer Gill but, I just had to do something about that new kid." Then I started to look at how Kenny was dressed. I asked Kenny, "Since when have you worn gang colors to school?"

Kenny's answer was shocking. He said," OG (my street name given to me by the students), I joined a gang over the summer break and I just had to stab that new kid because he was claiming his gang on my campus."

As I walked with Kenny to my waiting patrol car numerous emergency vehicles were on campus. Police cars, fire trucks and ambulances were on campus to assist. A crime scene was set up and officers were interviewing students that witnessed the stabbing.

School secretaries Bridget and Robin were calling parents and Principal Marjorie was again on the telephone informing school administrators and school district board members about the stabbing incident. Paramedics were with the other student tending to his stab wounds.

I asked Bridget who was the student with the stab wounds

and she informed me that he was a new student transferred in from Texas.

Bridget identified the student-stabbing victim as 17-year-old Mathew. Bridget went on to say that his mother was stationed in the Army at Camp Parks. Bridget did not know a lot about Mathew other than he and his mother just moved to California from Fort Hood, Texas.

It did not take her long but an angry Army mother wearing a camouflage utility uniform named Stacey was on campus looking for her son Mathew and looking for the kid that stabbed her son.

I walked over to talk with her to explain what was occurring regarding her son Mathew. Stacey was out of control and she wanted that other kid now. My old Marine Corp platoon sergeant days came back when I began to bark out to Stacey, "Stand down soldier! Get it together and stand down!"

She did not like it but she did listen to me. I told her that I was busy with an active crime scene and that the other student was arrested so I had to stay focused and maintain control to protect everyone.

I suggested that she should "get into the ambulance and go to the emergency room" with her son. I told Stacey that I would meet with her and Mathew at the hospital later and that I would keep her informed about my criminal investigation into the stabbing at school. Stacey took my suggestion and she got into the ambulance with her son Matthew.

Now, I was in charge of my crime scene. I learned in the police academy that the first officer on scene was in charge of a crime scene and I was the first officer to arrive. I started barking orders to get a confusing crime scene under control. I had officers already collecting evidence keep a tight control of all evidence collected. Did anyone ever hear of the OJ Simpson case?

I had detectives collect statements from witnesses to make sure all information was accurate. I had officers escort all teachers and their students to a safe area to re-unite students with their parents.

I briefed the PIO (Public Information Officer) on what probably occurred so that he could inform the press, which was converging on the scene with their news camera crews, as well as a group of politicians asking questions about the incident.

And finally, I had Officer Ramos escort Kenny to the police station for a Mirandized statement. I let everyone know that I was in charge of my crime scene. About three hours later it was all over at the school.

All the evidence was collected in the proper order including photos and videos. Detectives collected ten written statements from student witnesses. Kenny was safe at the police station where he was read his Miranda rights.

To my shock Kenny did not want to give detectives his formal statement until I arrived. Kenny told detectives he would not tell his story until I arrived because he knew I would treat him fair.

I brought Kenny a hamburger and a soda that I picked up at a local drive through fast food restaurant and I gave it to Kenny in the police department interview room. Even suspects get hungry.

The detectives left the room and only Kenny and I were there to talk. We sat next to each other eating burgers, enjoying a late lunch and talking about sports. When we were done with lunch I asked Kenny my first question about the stabbing.

I asked him, "What happened at school today Kenny?" His response was, "I had to do it today OG because he (Mathew) was all over social media telling everyone in town that he was going to kick my butt at school today" Kenny went on to say that Mathew was in a gang in Texas and that he heard that I joined a gang over the summer break. I just listened because Kenny had a lot to say.

My second question was, "Are you in a gang now Kenny?"

and Kenny told me "Yes, I joined a gang over the summer break after my cousin was shot and killed." I listened to Kenny and learned he went to visit family in Little Rock, Arkansas during the summer break. During his visit in Little Rock his first cousin was shot and killed by another local gang. One cousin died when the other local gang did a drive-by shooting as his cousins stood in their front yard.

Kenny told me he joined his family's gang to seek revenge for his cousin's death. In order to join the families gang Kenny and his cousins did a drive by shooting on the other local gang they suspected of killing their family member. Since participating in the drive-by shooting Kenny began wearing gang colors to show his family how proud he was to be a third generation gang member of the family gang.

Kenny admitted he began to brag about being a gang member on social media and that is when gang member Mathew threatened and challenged to fight Kenny.

Kenny said when he arrived at school today Mathew was there waiting for him. Students that knew about the fight were there waiting to see Kenny and Mathew fight as well. Mathew was wearing his gang colors and he approached Kenny asking him, "What are you going to do now punk? It is just you and me now" Kenny told me that he and Mathew dropped their backpacks and the fight was about to begin. Kenny said that is why he had a knife because he was expecting a fight with Mathew.

Kenny took out the knife and he was going to just show Mathew the knife but Mathew kept closing in on him making threats. Kenny admitted he stabbed Mathew twice in the lower torso area and he slashed Mathew's left arm as Mathew tried to run away.

I found Kenny to be very honest during his statement and very cooperative about the entire stabbing incident at school. I ended my conversation by telling Kenny that he had to go to Juvenile Hall for assault with a dangerous weapon.

I informed him that detectives might contact Little Rock Police Department to collect additional information about his gang activities in Arkansas. Kenny was not concerned because he told me that "no one will cooperate with the police in Arkansas" (that's called gang life in the hood).

Kenny said he understood he had to pay for what he did at school but he wanted me to explain everything to his grandmother. It was too late as the detective contacted her at her house before I arrived at the police station.

I drove over to the hospital to collect a written statement from Mathew. I asked Mathew if he was willing to tell me about the fight at school. Stacey began to speak for Mathew saying, "Of course Mathew is willing to talk because we want to file charges against the kid that stabbed him."

I asked Mathew my first question, "Mathew what happened at school today?" As Mathew began telling me his side of the story about the incident his mother Stacey interrupted with her version of the stabbing.

I told Stacey that I needed to hear from Mathew because he was there and she wasn't. I informed Stacey she was there only as an observer and not to interrupt Mathew during his statement. Stacey did not like my warning statement to her but she did stop interrupting Mathew for a while.

Mathew said, "I heard this kid wanted to fight me at school today and I was just standing there talking to a couple of girls when he just stabbed me with a knife."

I asked Mathew "How did you hear about the fight and why did you not report threats made against you?"

His response was "Kids at school told me this kid wanted to fight me and I don't know why." I asked Mathew "Who were the girls he was talking to at the time?" and his response was "I don't know their names because I'm new to the school."

Every question I asked was answered with he did not know or he did not have any idea about how or why the fight started.

I asked Mathew if he ever communicated with any of the other Dublin students on social media sites and if he was in a gang.

Before he could answer Stacey interrupted again and she wanted me to ask her son the right questions. Stacey said the right question was, "Did the kid that stabbed him at school today for no reason get arrested and did he go to juvenile hall?"

All of Mathew's statement was very brief and before he signed his formal statement I asked Mathew if all the information in his statement was true. Before Mathew could answer Stacey interrupted saying, "My son does not lie and everything he told you was the truth!"

I asked Mathew if he wanted to add or change anything in his statement and again he said "No." Mathew read and signed his statement. Once that was done Stacey asked, "Now what will happen?"

I informed Stacey and Mathew that I had ten statements from student witnesses and their version of what happened at school was the same version given by the suspect. I informed Mathew that he left a lot of information out of his statement and that crime victims usually offered more information to help their case.

I ended my interview saying the Chief of Police received a call from a Colonel Stevens, the commander of Camp Parks Army Reserve base and that I was instructed to contact the Colonel before I ended my shift of the day.

As I began to walk away from the hospital room I saw a scared look on Stacey and Mathew's face. Stacey was very angry and she asked me "Were you ever in the military, because you carry yourself different than any other cop?" and I answered, "Yes I was in the Marine Corps from 1969 to 1975." Stacey said, "That figures, you Marines think you are all a bunch of bad asses." My reply was, "We Marines don't think we are a bunch of bad asses, we Marines know we are a bunch of bad asses."(That felt good to say to Army Specialist Stacey).

Earlier I placed a long distant telephone call to the U.S. Army base at Fort Hood, Texas and I spoke with the on duty Military Provost and Police watch commander.

I informed the Military Police Lieutenant on duty that I was investigating a gang fight and stabbing in California and I asked the Lieutenant about former army dependent Mathew as he was involved. I asked the Lieutenant if he was aware that Mathew was claiming he was in a gang while living on the army base. The lieutenant told me that he would contact the commander of Camp Parks and brief him on my request for information about gangs on the base and about army dependent Mathew.

When I arrived at the police station Colonel Stevens was waiting for me. The MP Lieutenant from Fort Hood briefed the Colonel at Camp Parks and the Colonel told me "Yes the army was very aware of Mathew and his 40 gang member friends on the Fort Hood base." He was advised that Mathew and his gang friends caused a lot of troubles around the base canteen and the base theater every weekend.

Because of all their base gang problems, the base commander of Fort Hood transferred all the Army personnel and their army dependent brats to other army duty stations.

The Colonel ended saying "I never met Mathew but based on what I was told, I am surprised it took Mathew this long to get into trouble because I was told that Mathew was the main instigator when he was living on base in Texas." The Colonel said, "Now that I have all the pertinent information I plan on taking immediate corrective action first thing in the morning."

Investigators learned from Little Rock Police that Kenny and his family were involved in three other gang related assaults but no charges were filed against them as no one wanted to cooperate with law enforcement. (In street slang that is called life in the hood).

The Colonel arranged for the immediate transfer of Stacey and Mathew to another army base due to their involvement with gangs in the military. They were transferred out of the State of California before Kenny's trial began.

Kenny was found guilty of assault with a dangerous weapon with a gang enhancement and sentenced to five years with the California Youth Authority

I lost contact with Kenny's grandmother as she stopped participating in all school fund raising events as well as a lot of senior community activities.

It was a sad ending for a sad day in Dublin. Another case solved by Dublin Police and their SRO.

Chapter Twelve

THE BEVERAGE HEIST

I met with home economics teacher Holly at Dublin High School regarding suspected missing property. Holly stated after searching her classroom storage area she wanted to make a police report of missing donated property.

Holly stated the "Hanson Food Distributors" delivered 38 pallets of "Lost" energy drink. Each pallet contained about 40-10oz cans in assorted flavors. The 10oz cans are not sold in retail stores and are considered a special promotional item for the company. Holly said that all 38 pallets of the energy drinks were taken totaling 1520 cans.

Holly and other teachers searched the campus for the missing items and their search met with negative results. The school administration was notified of the stolen product and emails were sent to all school staff to be on the lookout for the missing product on campus.

Assistant Principal, Terry Young, received confidential information about the missing energy drinks. Student sources that wanted to remain anonymous due to possible retaliation, told the assistant principal that 12th grade Dublin High School student David and 12th grade Valley High School student Jennifer were responsible for taking the energy drinks from the home economics department.

The assistant principal was unable to speak with David or Jennifer as she had suspended them for flooding the student quad with water as a homecoming prank. The assistant principal said she would follow-up with the information when they returned to school.

I met with the assistant principal to follow-up on information regarding the stolen energy drinks and she asked me to stay as an observer while she questioned David about the stolen property.

She confronted David about the theft from the home economics department and he admitted taking the energy drinks from the school and he admitted that Jennifer assisted him with the theft.

David offered to return the energy drink but about 10 cases were missing as other high school students, many of them senior varsity football players, heard about the beverage theft and they stole the stolen property from him.

The assistant principal suspended David from school and contacted his mother at work by telephone informing her of the theft. I transported David to the police station for follow-up questions. David had many police contacts on and off campus with all his previous contacts for simple petty offenses.

After processing David, I drove to Valley High School and picked up Jennifer for follow-up questions. The principal at Valley High School spoke with the assistant principal from Dublin High School and they suspended Jennifer and notified her mother by telephone about the energy drink theft. Jennifer, like David, had numerous police contacts as well.

I read David and Jennifer their MIRANDA rights, which they acknowledged and they each agreed to give a written statement. In summary, David admitted seeing the energy drinks when he was leaving school one afternoon. Later that night David met with Jennifer and they decided to return to the campus in his pick-up truck and take the energy drinks as the energy drinks were going to be used as props for sophomore class homecoming skit.

David and Jennifer took the energy drinks to an abandoned house near Jennifer's home only as a "senior school prank." They began to tell other students about the theft and several students went to the abandoned house to steal the drinks from David and Jennifer. (That is different - someone stealing from the two original thieves).

David stated he and Jennifer decided to return the energy drinks late one night when the school was closed but several cases were missing.

Information continued to come into the assistant principals with other students being implicated. Many of the suspects were varsity football players.

Parents of many varsity football players volunteered to donate money to the school to pay for the energy drinks their sons were suspected of taking from David and Jennifer. (I think their sons were responsible for drinking stolen energy drinks. That's called a police clue).

The parents of David and Jennifer also agreed to pay for the stolen energy drinks, as the money that was to be raised in the energy drink sales was for the student fund.

David's and Jennifer's parents met with me at the police station again and David and Jennifer were released to their parents on a Notice to Appear. Their Notice to Appear in Juvenile Court was suspended until David and Jennifer completed a community service project. The school district was open to the community service project as they made a small profit from all the football players donating money to repay for the energy drinks. (I think their football coach had something to do with them wanting to donate money rather than face a suspension from school and losing time playing a game).

David's and Jennifer's parents were open to allowing their children to perform a community service project to repay their debt of wasted time to the school district and the city. I informed them that the City of Dublin was always looking for volunteers during the St. Patrick's Day weekend as the city held a parade and a street fair that was open to the public.

I told the parents that David and Jennifer could work at the Dublin Police Crime Prevention booth as our volunteers. (I often used juveniles with supervision problems to volunteer their time during the city's annual St. Patrick's Day parade and weekend street fair celebrations).

About one month later it was St. Patrick's Day and the festival was held in the Dublin City Hall area. Dublin Police had a Crime Prevention booth in the center of the festival. David and Jennifer were in the police booth to volunteer their time and labor as agreed.

At first they were not so eager to help but I explained their duties for the weekend. They slowly began to accept their responsibilities without a problem until it was time to wear the "McGruff the Crime Fighting Dog" costume. (Did I forget to tell them they had to wear the costume?)

David was tall and I thought he would fit in the costume without a problem. Jennifer was small and she had to adjust to fit in the costume.

I said to David that kids at the festival were looking for McGruff the crime fighting dog so he needed to get into the costume right away. At first he did not want to do it but I reminded him that he volunteered so I said, "David, get into the costume now because, kids are waiting for McGruff the crime fighting dog". Jennifer began to laugh at David until I reminded her that she was in the costume next.

David was sent to a private room and after a couple of minutes he walked out wearing the McGruff crime fighting dog costume.

I told David he did not have to say anything but just wave at little kids. Jennifer and I walked with David and we handed out coloring books, crayons colorful stickers for bicycles, pencils and pencil erasers to little kids.

When it was Jennifer's turn, David and I walked with her to again hand out school supplies to little kids.

At the end of the festival David and Jennifer told me they had a surprisingly good time because it made them feel good to help the community and help little kids.

Their community service was successful and their Notices to Appear were suspended indefinitely.

Another case solved by the assistant principal and the SRO.

Chapter Thirteen

TRAPPING KIDS WITH A KEYBOARD

One morning before I began my patrol shift I received an urgent call from Assistant Principal Madelyn Barns at Dublin High School. The call was regarding a student who was depressed and needed evaluation for an Emergency Psychiatric Detention. I immediately drove over to the high school and met with Assistant Principal Barns to collect additional information on her urgent call for service.

Barns informed me that a school counselor brought 11th grade student Danielle to her attention after Danielle told her counselor that she wanted to kill her mother in her sleep and commit suicide today.

Barns and I met with Danielle's counselor Kelly in the counselor's private office. While there, we spoke with Danielle about her claim of wanting to kill her mother and commit suicide.

Danielle confirmed she was depressed after several angry arguments with her mother over the weekend. Danielle did not want to tell us why she was angry with her mother other than, "My mother took my cell phone away and she is trying to ruin my life". Danielle began to cry and she refused to answer any other questions.

Kelly said Danielle told her she was depressed as it was nearing the one-year anniversary date of her brother's death. Danielle's brother died in a DUI accident.

I asked Assistant Principal Barns to telephone Danielle's

mother to first make sure she was still alive and not murdered in her sleep before I had to call another police officer to go to the residence.

Secondly and more importantly, to warn her mother that Danielle wanted to kill her. I also wanted her mother to not immediately come to the school, as Danielle might become violent seeing her mother on campus.

I placed a cellular telephone call to police emergency dispatchers and requested an ambulance for a "green sheet" (police code for 5150 H&S). California law, under Health and Safety Code 5150—Emergency Psychiatric Detention, allows police to place suspected suicidal subjects under a special detention for psychiatric evaluation for up to 72-hours.

Danielle said she tried to cut her wrist with a knife to end her life. I asked her to show me her wrists and I saw two long slightly open slash marks that appeared fresh on her left wrist. I searched Danielle's backpack for a weapon and Danielle told me she used a knife from her kitchen at home.

As we waited for the ambulance to arrive Danielle began to talk to Kelly and myself again. She told us that she had thoughts of killing her mother during the night numerous times. It was not until her mother checked her cell phone and then took the cell phone away that she really wanted to kill her mother.

I asked Danielle "Why did your mother take the cell phone away?" and Danielle answered, "Because she found a naked photo I took of myself and I was going to send it to my boyfriend." Now that little bit of news changed everything.

I asked Danielle "Why would you send your boyfriend a naked photo from your cell phone?" Her response was "because he is the only one that understands what I'm going through and he likes to listen to my troubles". I asked Danielle "What are your troubles?" Danielle said, "My mother is evil. She divorced my father and made him move to Washington State and now he has a new family without me. Then she did not help my brother with his problems and he died in a car accident. My mother just doesn't care about anyone but herself. She is just evil".

After listening to Danielle describe her mother, I just had to speak up. I started with "Are you telling me your boyfriend can't listen to your personal problems unless you are naked?" Danielle said, "No, he just asked if I was willing to send him a sexy photo, so I did to make him happy".

I told Danielle that, "I plan to come back to that question later." I went on and said, "I don't know why your mom and dad divorced but I do know of your brother's car accident. Being a police officer in a small town cops often discuss some of our cases. Your brother made the mistake of smoking weed (marijuana) with his friends at a party, drinking a lot of alcohol, then deciding to drive home on a rainy night, and losing control of his car and colliding with a large oak tree." Danielle just listened.

I went on and said, "That auto accident was not your mother's fault. You lost a brother but your mother just lost a son. Your mother may be trying to save her only surviving child, you, but you are not helping. Yes, your mother found that naked photo on your cell phone and she took the phone away from you. I bet your dad would do that too so, your mother was right when she took your cell phone."

Danielle did not answer or verbally respond to my comments but she did nod her head indicating yes as a non-verbal response. That's when we noticed the ambulance drivers standing at the office door.

I informed Danielle that I intended on sending her to see a psychiatrist for her depression and thoughts of suicide and that she was not under arrest.

I told Danielle, "Please talk to the psychiatrist to get help with your personal problems and thoughts of suicide because we all need you in our lives." To our shock Danielle said, "Thank you all for caring about me."

I placed Danielle on a 72-hour Emergency Psychiatric Detention per 5150 of the California Health & Safety Code and the EMS ambulance crew transported her to a hospital for a medical evaluation first. Protocol requires medical evaluation due to Danielle using a kitchen knife to slice her left wrist.

Assistant Principal Barns placed a telephone call to Danielle's mother and informed her of her daughter's detention status. Danielle was transported to Kaiser Hospital before she was transported to see the on-call psychiatrist.

Everyone did a great job in helping this troubled family and a depressed young student.

Another case solved by good school administrators and the SRO. (Now I have to locate Danielle's boyfriend to talk about that photo he asked her to send him).

Chapter Fourteen

THE ADMIRALS BOAT

It all started in Dublin when he was only fourteen years old but he just had to drive. A public commuter bus was waiting near the Dublin High School for additional students to cross the busy street, when the bus driver exited the bus to smoke a quick cigarette. The bus was just idling at the bus stop when Justin just had to drive.

Justin noticed the bus driver standing several feet behind the bus smoking his cigarette when he quickly scooted into the driver's seat and put the commuter bus into gear. Then Justin closed the doors and pulled away from the curb. The bus driver was in shock when he noticed his assigned commuter bus driving away in the number two lane without him. Students on the bus were in shock as well. The students thought "Justin can't drive this commuter bus because he is a student like me and he is in my third period class."

The driver went into panic mode, thinking: who is driving my bus? The driver began to chase after his bus but the bus continued to travel farther and farther away from the bus stop. How can I stop the bus from getting too far? What am I going to do?

I just happened to be in the area of the bus stop when I noticed the bus driver waving at me in a panic. I drove over to see what was the matter.

My bus is gone! I was waiting for students and someone stole my bus! "Where is the bus now" I asked and the bus driver pointed south and said "he is driving my route now with students on board the bus?" I instructed the bus driver to get into my police car and I said, tell me your route. As the bus driver gave me directions to his bus route I placed a call to my dispatcher instructing her that a public commuter bus was taken from the high school area and to advise all available patrol units to be on the lookout for a 40-foot commuter bus loaded with school students.

A few minutes after placing that emergency broadcast the bus driver and I noticed the commuter bus at a bus stop letting students off. The bus appeared to be picking up and dropping off passengers.

I activated my emergency lights and sirens stopping the commuter bus just feet before the next bus stop. The driver quickly bailed out of the patrol car and ran to the front door of the bus. I ran behind him to prevent any kind of physical confrontation between the assigned bus driver and the unknown bus driver.

The unknown bus driver was a student. I ordered the student bus driver off the bus and I placed him in the back of my patrol car. The unknown student identified himself as Justin.

Additional patrol units arrived and we entered the bus to make sure all the students were unharmed. Many of them thought it was funny that their friend at school stole a commuter bus and gave them all a fun ride. Many of them could not wait to tell their friends at school the next day about Justin driving off with a commuter bus.

I returned to my patrol car and Justin tried to explain his actions. His first spontaneous statement to me was "I just have to drive." I told Justin he was lucky he was not involved in an accident because he drove the commuter bus over fifteen city blocks before I stopped him. Justin replied with "I ride that bus every day and I know the route, I even dropped passengers off and let passengers on without a problem. I watch the bus driver all the time and I just have to drive."

I drove Justin over to the police station and called his mother Janice at work. As we waited for his mother to arrive I began processing Justin for grand theft of a motor vehicle (commuter bus).

Janice told me she suspected Justin was sneaking out late at night driving her SUV around town. Janice stated she would mark her car tires and the driveway with chalk and she noticed the tires were not in the same chalk marks in the morning when she went off for work. Janice confronted Justin about his unauthorized late night driving and he would tell her that he "had to drive."

Because Justin was fourteen years old he was sent to youth court. The youth court gave Justin over a hundred hours of community service. Justin volunteered to wash police cars and public utility trucks as part of his community service hours.

Justin was very quiet for a long time after completing his community service hours. Things changed when Justin was sixteen years old.

Justin took an interest in a couple of girls that lived a couple of streets off his street. The two girls, Stacy and Tracy, were sisters that had a reputation around school as being "party girls".

Justin wanted to impress the party girl sisters by bragging to them about his fast cars, his SUV, his motorcycle and his sport boat. The sport boat caught their attention. The sisters had real skimpy bikinis and they wanted to cruse the delta wearing their skimpy bikinis in a cool ski and sport boat. What will Justin do?

Justin walked past a cool looking ski boat every day after school. The boat was the property of a neighbor that lived across the street and the boat was just sitting there in front of his neighbor's house. Justin just wanted to borrow the boat to take out a couple of socially active sisters in skimpy bikinis.

Justin knew the neighbor was working on the weekends and that he had not taken the boat out in a couple of months. Justin knew the neighbor would leave for work at five am and he would not return until after 6pm in the afternoon. Justin had a plan.

Justin thought he could borrow the boat early and be back with the boat before the neighbor noticed the boat was even missing. The timing was perfect because Justin's mother was out of town that weekend and her SUV was just sitting in the driveway.

That day Justin was up early and he noticed his neighbor leave for work. Now, time to borrow his neighbor's boat and pick up the sisters for a delta cruse. Justin had his mother's SUV and everything was a go. In a short while Justin and the two girls were off to the delta. Justin could not wait to see the skimpy bikinis the sisters had.

Justin was able to launch the boat into the delta without a problem and he was able to start the boat and cruse the delta. So far so good for now.

After a couple of hour's cruising the delta it was time to return home. Now we have a problem. Getting the sport boat back on the trailer was difficult for Justin. Other boaters were waiting to launch their boats and Justin tried to figure out how to secure the boat and leave. Justin did not want to ask for help because he had two girls that thought he knew all about fast cars, motorcycles and boats.

Another problem was that boaters were waiting to take their turn. They did not understand the delay. One of the boaters waiting for Justin to secure his boat on the trailer just happened to be a boat mechanic working for the Mercury Boat Company in the City of Dublin.

The mechanic told his friends that he recognized the Mercury M series ski and sports boat and that the sixteen-year old kid did not own the boat. The mechanic told his friends that he repaired the boat and that he knew the boat owner. Did the owner loan out his boat? The mechanic wrote down the license plate number of the SUV just in case the boat owner wanted to know who took his boat.

After what seemed like hours Justin was able to tie the boat down to the trailer and he was off towards the freeway.

From the side view mirrors of the SUV, Justin could see the boat was not as secure as he thought. The trailer swayed from side to side and Justin thought the boat would come off and land on the freeway. If the boat landed on the freeway the two girls would have a lot to tell at school and he would not be cool in the eyes of everyone at school.

Justin pulled over to the shoulder of the road and tried again to secure the boat to the trailer. No luck.

Justin unhitched the trailer and left the boat and trailer on the side of the freeway. Justin told the two girls that the trailer had a flat tire and he had to return later for the trailer with another tire.

Justin was able to get the two girls home and they all started to party. Justin lost track of time and forgot to return to the abandoned boat on the freeway and most important get the boat back to his neighbor.

When the neighbor returned home from work he noticed right away that his boat was missing. After all, the boat was parked in front of his house when he left for work that morning. The boat's owner called the police to report the boat as stolen.

At the same time the California Highway Patrol inspected the abandoned boat and trailer and they marked the boat for freeway removal. Emergency dispatchers told the Dublin police officer taking the police report, that the CHP located the boat on the freeway and marked the boat for immediate removal.

The owner was given the boat's location on the freeway and he decided to go recover and retrieve his property.

The owner was not sure if his boat was damaged so he towed his boat to the Mercury Boat Company and left the boat in the back lot as the company was closed for the weekend.

On Monday morning the owner of the boat repair shop

noticed the familiar boat in the back lot. Soon the boat mechanic arrived for work and again he saw the same boat he had repaired numerous times and that he had seen on the delta over the weekend. A big break in the case.

The mechanic told the shop owner about the sixteen-year old kid with the boat on the delta and he wrote down the license number of the SUV that was attached to the boat trailer.

The boat owner was contacted with the good news as was the police. It didn't take long and the police were on their way to Justin's house.

Justin was a familiar face since he washed many police cars on his community service. With his mother present, Justin admitted taking the boat and leaving the boat on the side of the freeway. Justin also admitted the reason he took the boat was he wanted to show off for the two sisters wearing skimpy bikinis.

Justin's mother asked him why would he take a neighbor's boat? Justin's reply was the usual "I just have to drive and I don't care what I drive."

Justin was again processed for grand theft auto but he was not eligible for youth court as he already attended youth court once and his youth court rehabilitation plan failed. Justin's case was sent to juvenile court for final adjudication.

A couple of years had passed when an investigator that had a question about Justin called me. Justin was now over 18 years old and he was a suspect in an auto embezzling case.

Justin was working as a car washer in an auto-detailing department for a large auto dealership. Justin was doing well until the auto dealership noticed one new car was missing from its inventory.

The detective had a list of employees and he noticed Justin's name on the list. I briefed the detective on my history with Justin and the detective called Justin to the police station for an interview.

Justin admitted he took the new car after he detailed the car for a showroom display. Justin began by taking the new car for a quick spin around the block and that was all it took; Justin had to take the car on a short field trip to Lake Tahoe. The detectives recovered the new car at a girlfriend's house.

Justin ended his confession with the detectives saying, "I just have to drive."

Chapter Fifteen

SAMANTHA IS DIFFERENT

On a Monday morning, I received a call from Dublin High School counselor Larry Carpenter regarding a possible case of child abandonment or suspected child neglect. I met with Larry and he told me two female students came to him to report in confidence that a friend of theirs was possibly kicked out of her house by her parents and that their 17-year old friend was possibly homeless.

The two girls gave their friend's name as Samantha. Larry added that sometimes Samantha's friends at school called her by her nickname "Sam" for short.

Larry asked me how we should handle this case. I told him that we should just call Sam out of her class and ask her if she was homeless. If she said yes, we can come up with a plan to help her. Sam was called out of class and the investigation began.

Larry ran Sam's name in the school computer and saw her grades were good and she was on track to graduate later in the school year.

When Samantha arrived in Larry's office she had a scared and curious look on her face when she saw me sitting there. Larry said, "Don't worry Sam, you're not in trouble and Officer Gill is one of the good guys." She had a look of relief on her face and she sat down in a chair next to Larry.

I had a direct approach when talking with some students and

I asked Sam if she was okay. Then I asked her if she was homeless and living on the streets. Sam said, "No, I'm living with a friend for now." I asked her if she was having trouble at home because her friends were very concerned about her safety. Again Sam said, "No problems at home, I just needed some space from my parents, so my friend offered me a place to stay for a couple of weeks."

I said, "We just have to confirm that you're staying with a school friend and it is okay with your parents and your friends' parents so let's give your mom a call."

Suddenly Sam started to become concerned and she did not want us to contact her mom Elizabeth. I even offered to put her mom on speakerphone so that she could hear my conversation with her mom.

Sam was now so upset she almost started to cry. Larry stood up and closed the curtains to his office windows so Sam could have a little privacy. Larry and I did not understand why suddenly Sam did not want us to contact her mom. It was looking like Sam did not tell us the whole story about her living with a school friend. I asked Sam to tell us the whole story about her parents so we could help her.

It took Sam a while to compose herself but she finally agreed to tell us her secret. Sam said, "What I am about to tell you is embarrassing for me so give me a minute" and I said, "We won't judge anyone for making a mistake if a mistake was made." Sam came out and told us her secret. Sam said in a low tone that she was gay.

I did not know much about gay issues but I read that gay teen life in high school was not easy. Gay teens are the ones that are most common targets for bullying. Gay teens suicide rates are higher than any other youth groups. And many gay teens struggle to find acceptance at their school, at home and within. Once Sam opened up she began to tell us her story and about her home life.

Sam told us her mother re-married about six years ago and her stepfather, Ken, was hard on her. Sam's stepfather was a strict religious Christian and he did not understand why Sam chose not to participate in more family church activities.

Sam did not know how to talk with her religious Christian stepfather, as when she attended church with the family all she heard from people there was that gay people are doomed to hell if they don't change their behavior and embrace their church beliefs.

Sam's mother would say that there were no gays on her side of the family and she often had thoughts of abomination. Sam would often hear her stepfather say gays should all be lined up against a wall and shot because gays have a disease. Many members of the church her parents attended would often say AIDS is a disease gays deserved because they lost their way with the church.

Her mother Elizabeth and her stepfather Ken had two children together and she now has a five-year-old stepbrother named Jedediah and a three-year-old stepsister Amaras. Sam felt that her siblings got all the attention from her parents.

Sam had a tough time understanding what was happening to her young body but she knew she was different than the other girls in school. She said she did not have an attraction to boys but she had an attraction to other girls. She just did not know how to start a conversation with anyone about her having possible lesbian feelings. What made her situation even more difficult was she felt that her parents did not want to talk about it. Maybe they did not understand it as well.

Sam went on to say things began to change for her one day when she received a text message on her cell phone from someone saying, "Hello, I'm pretty sure you are gay and I like you because I'm gay too." Sam was pretty sure she had kept her feelings a secret. She was in shock that the text message referred to her as being gay because again she thought she was keeping her feelings a secret. Soon other text messages were received on her cell phone until she decided to meet the sender.

That text message led to her meeting the sender in a location away from school. Sam was surprised to find out that the text message sender was a girl she had known since they were both in the 8th grade. After a couple of months, the two girls began a secret friendship.

Sam's mother and her secret friend's mother were work friends so the two girls would just hang out, like a couple of schoolgirls. The two girls went to the movies together and sometimes they did homework together. The two mothers believed and understood that they were just school friends.

Then one day when Sam and her secret friend were home alone listening to music it happened. The two girls began to kiss. The kissing led to them touching each other, which led to them taking off each other's clothing. Sam said it started out very innocently but things got out of control.

Sam did not hear anyone in the house at the time but suddenly her stepbrother Jedediah opened her bedroom door. He yelled out for his dad Ken when he caught his stepsister and her friend lying on her bed without clothes.

Sam's stepfather was very angry when he entered the room. Sam and her school friend were busy putting their clothes back on. Sam told us her stepfather "Just blew up and started yelling at the both of them." Sam and her school friend were very embarrassed about the incident and how her stepfather learned about her secret and private life.

Sam told us her stepfather began quoting fire and brimstone scripture from the Bible and he kept ranting and raving about them going to hell. Ken said she should be ashamed at what her stepbrother just witnessed. He called her mother Elizabeth at work to tell her all about the incident in Sam's bedroom.

Sam's stepfather wanted her to leave the family now because he felt that Sam was not a good example for her much younger step siblings.

When her mother returned home from work she too joined her stepfather and they both began to rant and rave about what occurred earlier.

Sam told us she packed a few things and she called another school friend and asked for a place to stay until she was able to figure out what to do.

Sam had an after school job as a part-time grocery bagger with the local Safeway store so she earned a little money to support herself. Sam's friend also worked part-time with the same grocery store. The friend asked her mother if Sam could stay at her house and her mother agreed to allow Sam to sleep on the family sofa.

I suggested Larry contact Sam's mother Elizabeth and request a special conference to discuss Sam's future. I also suggested Sam make contact with the student president of the school's LGBT club so Sam could get support and ideas on how to handle her parents, other students and her feelings.

The LGBT club had an adult sponsor who had experience with students who come out and admit they were gay. Sam told us she was open to that idea and she said she could use new school friends now. After meeting with the LGBT club on campus Sam told us she was happy to learn that there were other gay students to support her at school.

Sam's mother was at home with the day off and she agreed to meet with us within an hour. Larry and I came up with ideas on how to approach Sam's mother regarding a very sensitive subject.

When Sam's mother, Elizabeth arrived, I again used the direct approach and told Elizabeth we know all about the incident that occurred in Sam's bedroom with her secret friend. Elizabeth confirmed it was a shock for her and her husband to learn about Sam's secret the way it happened.

Larry said, "Sam is a good student that is so close to graduation so let's work together to help her finish school and go off to college." We all agreed to work together and help Sam.

During our special meeting Sam returned to Larry's office after meeting with the LGBT president and mom and daughter started to talk with each other for the first time since her stepfather wanted her to leave.

We called the friend's parent, identified as Veronica, where Sam was sleeping on their family sofa. Veronica agreed to allow Sam to continue living in her home until after graduation. Sam offered to pay Veronica for the room and board through her part time job with Safeway. The plan was coming together and everything appeared to work out.

Sam's mother had a concern with Sam walking home alone late at night after work. Veronica agreed to pick up Sam after work but Veronica could not guarantee a ride home every night. Sam said, "I may be able to get a ride from some of my friends and I can work it out."

Everyone left the meeting feeling good and Sam and her mother Elizabeth began to hug each other and cry. Even though Elizabeth did not totally understand or agree with Sam's sexual orientation, Sam was still her first-born daughter.

I would check on Sam through Larry every now and then and Sam was on schedule to graduate and attend college. Transportation was still a problem because Sam did not have a driver's license and no plans to purchase a car.

There was a senior citizen that lived near Dublin High School and he would always honk his car horn and wave at me whenever he saw me patrolling around the high school. This was his daily routine.

On this particular day I drove down his street and I noticed a bicycle in his front yard with a for sale sign on it. The owner was asking only $20 for a new looking ten-speed bicycle. The bicycle was in good shape and did not appear to be used or worn down.

Floyd Gill

I pulled over to the curb and I got out of my patrol car to inspect the bicycle that was for sale. The senior citizen met me on the sidewalk and for the first time we spoke with each other, not just honking and waving at each other.

His name was Hans and he told me he came to the US in 1945 when he was twelve years old and that he was a holocaust survivor from Poland. Hans had a lot to talk about the holocaust because he lost a lot of family in concentration camps in war torn Poland.

Hans told me he was pro-police and he told me he felt safe and comfortable with having a police officer about a block away from his house every day. That was the reason he would honk his car horn and wave to me everyday when he saw me.

I told Hans that I had a young female student that needed some type of transportation home because she worked at a local grocery store and walked home late at night. I reached into my pocket and took out a $20 bill.

Hans took off the for sale sign and he tore the sign in half. He then said, "Just give the bicycle to the girl so she can get home safe." I again offered to pay for the bicycle but Hans refused to take my money.

I told him that I would have the girl receiving his generous gift write him a thank you letter. I informed Hans he may see his bicycle if he ever shopped at the Safeway store as she was a bagger that worked after school. I also told him that she planned on attending college and the bicycle would come in handy when she left for college.

I placed the bicycle into the backseat of my patrol car and I drove over to the high school campus to give the bicycle to Sam. She was happy and surprised to receive a bicycle and she remembered customer Hans shopping in the grocery store.

After graduation from Dublin High School Sam left the Bay Area and enrolled at the University of California Santa Barbara.

I ran into her mother Elizabeth a couple of years later and she informed me that Sam was doing well in college and Sam was happy.

Another case solved by the SRO and a little community policing.

Chapter Sixteen

A REAL WAR HERO

It was a Memorial Day weekend and there was no school that day with the Dublin School District so I was assigned a regular patrol beat for the day. Almost everything was closed due to the holiday except gas stations, fast food restaurants and department stores.

Traffic through town was very light, all the schools were closed for the day and the police radio was almost silent. It was a good day to go to work.

I drove down a lot of streets and I waved at a lot of citizens. Since there was no school a lot of school kids waved and wanted me to stop. I carried a lot of plastic stickers and I gave out a lot of community service props. The kids loved to collect that kind of stuff.

It was around 10:00 am when I drove down one street and I noticed three young boys, about 8 to 10 years old, waving me down. They had a golden retriever dog with a rope around his collar. They appeared to be excited about something so I pulled over to the curb to see what they wanted. They all told me that they found this dog wandering around the neighborhood. The boys told me they were afraid a passing car would hit the stray dog.

The dog was very friendly and he had a tag on his dog collar. The dog's name was "Buddy" and the address listed on the tag was about three blocks from my current location.

125

I opened the back door to my patrol car and Buddy the dog jumped in the back seat without a command to do so. I told the boys they did a good job by rescuing Buddy and that I was going to take Buddy back home.

The boys began to smile and as a reward I gave each boy a plastic "Junior Police Officer" badge and official plastic police stickers for their bicycles. I had the boys line up and raise their right hands.

With their hands raised, I performed an official street junior police swearing in ceremony asking each boy to do well in school, look both ways when they cross the street, eat all their vegetables, always brush their teeth and to always listen to their parents and teachers. They all swore to do just that and now they were official junior police officers. Their smiles were contagious.

I drove over to the address listed on Buddy's dog tag and I noticed the side gate near the garage was open. Maybe that is how Buddy was able to leave his yard. (That is called a police clue).

I opened the back door to my police car and Buddy quickly ran through the gate without a command to do so. Buddy was back home.

I closed the gate and made sure it was locked. I walked to the front door and rang the doorbell. After a couple of minutes there was no answer to the doorbell.

I left a business card in the front door jamb. I wrote on the back of the business card in small letters that their dog Buddy left the back yard and three boys caught him. If additional information was needed to call the police dispatcher number on the front of the card.

Buddy was safe at home, I had three newly sworn junior police officers on duty and it was still a good day to work.

Now the police radio was active with the report of an accident in the center of town. The traffic officer answered the call and was enroute to the accident. I began to travel in that direction just in case traffic control was needed.

When I arrived I noticed a tan colored Buick had crashed into a power pole and all electrical power, including traffic lights, was out for at least eight blocks in that area. Two fire trucks were on scene checking for gas leaks and downed power lines. The ambulance activated emergency lights and sirens and was leaving before I arrived on the scene.

I was told the driver was taken to the hospital and may not survive. The traffic officer and I were the senior deputies on duty that day so the two rookie deputies were given traffic control duties. Seniority pays.

When the ambulance crew arrived at the hospital they informed the emergency dispatcher that the elderly driver of the Buick was deceased. The sergeant called me over for a special detail. I was called to make a special "Death Notification".

Since the two rookies never had that type of duty before I was selected for this special detail. Seniority again.

The registered owners full name and address was on the car registration stored in the car glove box compartment.

The traffic officer briefed me on his accident investigation. The elderly male driver was waiting for the traffic light on the corner of Dublin Blvd. and Golden Gate Drive. That was a very busy intersection in the center of town.

The driver had just left the "Great Western Savings and Loan" located on the south side of the street at that intersection. While waiting at the traffic signal the driver suffered a heart attack. During the heart attack the driver accelerated through the intersection.

The driver struck the power pole located on the north side of the section. The downed power line caused a massive power outage for all the businesses in the area.

The fire department responded and extricated the elderly male driver that was not responding. Paramedics began CPR and the ambulance crew transported the driver to Valley Medical Care hospital in Pleasanton.

The trauma team at the hospital were unable to resuscitate the driver and he was pronounced deceased by the on duty physician.

We noticed the owners were Henry and Helen with an address in the City of San Ramon. The street listed on the registration ran on the border of San Ramon and the City of Dublin. I drove through that neighborhood before but I never had a call for service there.

As I drove through the neighborhood I noticed it was an older community with homes that housed a lot of senior citizens. I located Henry's street and I stopped in front of his house. I got out of the patrol car and I stood in the street for a couple of minutes to gather my thoughts.

As I stood in the street, I noticed a LOL (Little Old Lady) approaching me. She asked, "Is everything OK officer?" I answered by asking her "Do you know Henry and Helen that live at this address?" She replied, "Why yes, they have lived here for over 40 years like all of us".

I told her that I was here to give Helen some bad news about Henry. I told her that "Henry had a heart attack in the City of Dublin and Henry is not with us anymore". The LOL said, "Oh my, that's terrible news."

I asked her if she was a friend of Helen because Helen needed a friend right now. She told me her name was Ruth and that she would go inside with me to help Helen. As we both stood in the street a second LOL walked up to us wanting to know if everything was all right.

Before I could answer her Ruth said, "Oh Beatrice, this officer is here to see Helen. Henry had a heart attack and he's gone." Beatrice said, "Oh no, that's awful news, poor Helen."

For some unknown reason the two LOL began to hug me in the middle of the street. That was unexpected and weird.

Ruth told Beatrice that she was going to join Helen after I told her about Henry. Beatrice said, "I want to be with Helen too so I'll go with you." Now I have two friends to help Helen.

The three of us walked to the front door and I rang the doorbell. A LOL answered the front door and I asked her if she was Helen. She answered, "Yes I'm Helen." Before I could inform her of Henry's passing Ruth and Beatrice said in unison, "Oh Helen, Henry had a heart attack and now he's gone, we're so sorry."

Helen stepped forward and she began to hug me in the doorway. Ruth and Beatrice joined in for a group hug. Again that was unexpected and weird.

Helen invited me in and she offered me a cup of coffee. I declined the coffee but asked for a glass of water. Helen told me that Henry wanted to go to the City of Livermore to see the Memorial Day air show celebrations. The show was being held at the Livermore airport. Henry read in the newspaper and learned that a B17 bomber was going to be on display. Henry flew B17 bombers during WWII.

Henry wanted to go to the bank in Dublin before going to the airport. Helen said, "I told Henry he had enough money but he was stubborn and wanted to go to the bank first." Helen last saw Henry backing out of the driveway on his way to the air show. Helen said, "I felt something was going to happen today but Henry wanted to go."

Ruth and Beatrice offered to make me cookies to go with a cup of coffee. I declined but they insisted on baking cookies.

Helen asked me to stay until her son arrived. Henry and Helen had a son named Andrew that was a Lieutenant Colonel stationed at Travis Air Force Base in Fairfield. Helen escorted me to Henry's office and I called the Lieutenant Colonel using Henry's telephone.

I informed Andrew that his dad had a heart attack and he died at the hospital. Andrew asked if I would stay with his mother until he arrived and I informed him that I would. The Lieutenant Colonel would have to claim his dad's body and make arrangements for his dad's funeral.

After the telephone call I began to look around Henry's office. I saw a lot war memorabilia and photos of Henry and his aircrew from WWII. Henry appeared to be quite a bomber pilot with a lot of war stories to tell. I left and returned to the dining room.

As I waited in the dining room two LOM (Little Old Men) came over looking for their wives. Eighty-two-year-old Donald and eighty-three-year-old Roy were looking for their wives. Eighty-one-year-old Ruth was married to Donald and eighty-four-year-old Beatrice was married to Roy.

Both Donald and Roy wanted to know why their wives were here in Henry and Helen's home with Helen. I informed Donald and Roy that Henry had a heart attack and that Henry passed on.

Donald asked me, "Did Henry get to see the air show" and I said, "No, Henry had a heart attack after leaving the bank in Dublin." Then Donald and Roy just sat down at the dining room table and Roy took out a deck of pinnacle cards and began shuffling the cards.

Ruth walked over and gave Donald and Roy a cup of coffee. Of course Ruth gave me a cup of coffee as well.

After a couple of minutes Donald told me he served in the Navy on a destroyer and Roy told me he was in the Army with a tank division. Roy asked me if I ever served in the military. I responded saying, "Yes, I volunteered for the Marines and I served in Vietnam."

They were three old combat warhorses with a lot of stories to tell about the good old days when they were young men. Roy dealt me a hand in the pinnacle game.

Time went by and before you knew it Helen's son was at the front door. Helen walked over to tearfully hug him and Ruth and Beatrice joined in for another group hug.

The Lieutenant Colonel walked over and shook my hand. He

and I walked to Henry's office and I briefed him on the accident, the name of the tow company that stored his father car and where and how to claim his father's body for burial. The lieutenant colonel was grateful that I was able to stay with his mother and her friends and he thanked me and the police department for their work.

Before leaving Henry's office I said, "I was in your dad's office using the telephone earlier and as I looked around his office, I saw that your dad was quite a pilot during World War II due to all the decorations he earned." His response was "Yes, they don't make them like my old man anymore."

It was time to leave and I began walking towards the front door. I told Helen "Goodbye and good luck" and before I knew it she began hugging me in the hallway. Ruth and Beatrice saw Helen and they joined in for a final group hug.

Then Beatrice said, "Wait, I have something for you and the others officers at the police station." She walked to the kitchen and returned with a large paper bag filled with over three dozen handmade oatmeal raisin cookies. I said goodbye to Donald and Roy but they continued to drink coffee, eat fresh oatmeal cookies and play pinnacle.

When I walked out to my patrol car I placed the bag of cookies in the front seat. That's when I heard the sound of a low flying airplane. I looked to my left and saw a World War II bomber overhead. It was loud, slow and flying directly overhead towards my patrol car and me.

I kept looking at the airplane as I walked to the driver's side of the car. I could see the old bomber was going to fly directly over Henry's house.

I said, "Henry, it looks like your ride is here." Soon the bomber was close enough for me to read the number on the rear tail of the airplane. I saw the number 85 on the rear tailgate side of the airplane. Henry was 85 years old.

I gave Henry a final military salute. I stood at attention and gave the old airplane flying over me a sharp military salute (A sign of respect) and I said, "God bless you Henry. A job well done pilot. Rest in peace."

It was a good day to work.

Chapter Seventeen

WELCOME HOME SOLDIERS

I received a call from Mark Alcott, the Dean of Students at Dublin High School regarding students suspected of being in possession of alcohol on campus. Alcott is the Dean of Students for 9th and 12th grade students. I met with him to collect additional information on his call for police service.

Alcott stated concerned parent Julie came to school to report that her 15-year-old daughter stole a full bottle of vodka from home and that her daughter brought the bottle of vodka to Dublin High School to share with her friends.

Julie told Alcott that she was checking her daughter's computer "myspace.com" account (before Facebook) when she discovered entries made on the home computer indicating her daughter was telling her friends at school that she stole the vodka from home and wanted to share the bottle with her friends at school.

Julie confronted her daughter Barbie at home and was able to obtain a full confession about the stolen alcohol. Julie escorted her daughter to school to assist Alcott with his school investigation. Alcott and Julie were able collect the names of the other students involved in consuming the vodka on campus.

It came out that Barbie stole the vodka from a welcome home party held at the Camp Parks Army Base. Barbie's family lives on base at Camp Parks and her father is stationed on the army base. Barbie's father, Joe had just returned to Dublin after serving a tour of duty with the army in Iraq. All the adults were celebrating Joe's return home when Barbie slipped a full bottle of vodka away from the welcome home party. After the party Barbie got on her myspace.com chat room and informed her friends at school that she stole the vodka.

During PE class, Barbie shared the stolen vodka with her friends Cindy and Amy. Alcott suspended Barbie from school for bringing vodka alcohol to school and released her to her mother.

Alcott immediately called Cindy and Amy to his office for an interview to follow-up on the information collected earlier from Barbie. Alcott asked me to observe and assist him with the interviews.

Cindy was confronted with the information we had and she admitted she drank some vodka during her PE class and that Barbie brought the vodka to school. Alcott called her mother Ann and requested a special conference at school to discuss the drinking incident. Cindy was suspended from school for consuming alcohol during class.

Amy was confronted with the information we had and she admitted she also drank vodka during her PE class with the other three girls. Alcott called her father Andy and requested a special conference at school to discuss the incident. Amy was suspended from school for consuming alcohol during class.

It came out that Barbie's younger sister Jasmine was also involved and she covered for her older sister when her mother began the investigation at home. Alcott placed another telephone call back to Julie and requested a second special conference to discuss the new information collected from the prior interviews with Cindy and Amy.

A second special conference was held with parent Julie and her two daughters Barbie and 14-year-old Jasmine. Jasmine admitted she covered for her older sister and knew about the alcohol consumption in PE class.

Alcott suspended Jasmine from school for defiance and disruption of school activities as she helped her older sister Barbie and deliberately misled the investigation conducted by her mother and Alcott.

All four juveniles were reprimanded and released to their parents with a pending referral for a community service project as part of their discipline when they returned to school from their suspension.

The parents were in full support of community service because they did not want their daughters or their friends drinking at an early age.

Another case solved by responsible and concerned parents and the SRO.

Chapter Eighteen

TRAPPING KIDS WITH A KEYBOARD

I was working an overtime assignment at the I-MAX movie theater in Dublin on a busy Saturday night. The position was a high visibility-walking beat so that patrons could see a police presence in the area.

I was with my beat partner Mark when two students recognized me as their School Resource Officer. They rushed over to me to get my attention. As they walked over to me I noticed one girl was crying.

I recognized these two fifteen-year-old female students and I was happy they saw me walking in front of the movie theater. They told me they were in trouble and that they did something wrong.

One female told me, "Officer Gill, I'm in trouble because I made a serious mistake and I need your help right now." I told her to calm down and of course I would help her. I asked her, "What is the matter?"

She said, "First, I'm on restriction and I'm not supposed to be out." (That was her first mistake. Lying to her mother). My response was "Let's work through that problem later but why are you so upset?" She went on to say she "sent dirty pictures on the Internet to a boy I was chatting with but I just found out he is a grown man."

To comply with California Penal Code 293 the student's real name is confidential and in this story she will be identified as

Jane Doe. The law allows victims of sex crimes or domestic violence confidentiality status. Jane Doe's school friend will not be identified to maintain privacy and to help keep Jane's true identity confidential.

Jane said, "I met this boy name Frank on the Internet and he asked me to sneak out tonight to meet him at the I-Max movie theater." She went on to say "We were chatting on the Internet website MySpace (Before Facebook) and he told me that he was 17 years old with a new car and he lived in Stockton."

Jane said, "That was the reason me and my friend snuck out of the house to meet Frank." Jane and her school friend knew it was wrong to lie to their mothers and sneak out of their safe house but they did not think it would take a long time to finally meet Frank in person.

As I collected additional information Jane stated the plan called for her to meet Frank inside the movie theater during the movie "The Hobbit."

Jane was instructed by Frank to walk into the movie theater using the south door and then walk ten rows from the door. After ten rows from the door Jane was to take a seat in the center of the row.

Jane told me she and her friend did just as they were instructed by Frank and they sat waiting for a 17-year-old boy named Frank. The soft theater lights were still on as they waited. As Jane and her friend waited, an adult male wearing a London Fog type raincoat sat down next to Jane.

That is when Jane heard the adult male say, "Hello Jane, I've been waiting for you." Jane looked at the man and was in shock. Jane said she just froze and did not know what to do.

A couple of minutes later the theater lights lowered and movie commercials began to play. The adult male leaned over and said to Jane, "I've really enjoyed chatting with you on the computer."

Jane told me she told her friend that "they had to go" but her friend either did not hear or did not understand why. That's when the adult male took Jane's right hand and he placed her hand on his lap under his raincoat.

Jane stated she panicked and told her friend that she "had to go to the restroom now!" Jane stood up and she and her friend quickly left for the restroom.

Once in the theater lobby Jane told her friend that the unknown adult was Frank and that he took her hand and placed her hand on his lap under his raincoat. The two girls decided to leave the movie theater when they happened to see my patrol partner Mark and I walking on a foot patrol outside of the movie theater.

I asked Jane if the unknown male was still inside the movie theater and she replied "No, because that's him walking right over there." I noticed Jane was pointing at an adult male wearing a London Fog style raincoat approximately twenty feet away from us. I asked Jane, "Is that the man you were talking about?" and she said, "Yes that's him, I thought I was meeting Frank".

I quickly approached the male adult and I detained him for further questioning. The adult male made a spontaneous statement and said, "I just met that little girl and I accidentally touched her hand."

Jane positively identified the subject I was detaining as the man that called her by name, had a brief conversation about her on the Internet and later he took her hand and placed her hand under his raincoat.

Jane told us that she had been chatting with a Frank for several weeks and Frank asked her several times to meet in person. Jane said she was completely fooled into thinking she was going to meet a 17-year-old. She was in shock to find out Frank was actually an adult male.

I placed the adult subject in my patrol car and I continued my field investigation. The adult male was identified as 56-year-old Richard and Richard was approximately 5' 10", bald, weighing about 340 pounds. He was wearing a khaki raincoat with a t-shirt and shorts under the raincoat. It was a cool evening and Richard was sweating profusely.

Richard was such a large man that I had to use two sets of handcuffs to secure him. I placed Richard in the rear of my partner's patrol car and his placement was a real tight fit for him. I transported Jane and her friend to the patrol station to contact their parents.

We learned that Richard was a single man with no spouse or dependents and that Richard worked as a bank executive for a major bank. Richard's job called for him to conduct bank business all over the US and in foreign countries.

My partner Mark transported Richard to the police station for possible processing. Richard was told he was being detained for further investigation of Penal Code section 311.6 — Engaging in Obscene Material to a Minor. After being informed of the possible charges, Richard was read his Miranda rights. If additional information collected by Jane and her friend gave probable cause Richard would later be incarcerated in the county jail for suspected child pornography, enticing a child for sex by way of computer and contributing to the delinquency of a minor, as Jane and her friend were enticed to sneak out of their house.

Once they were comfortable at the patrol station Jane said, "I have not told you everything." I told Jane, I needed to know everything and that I would not judge her for making a mistake. I said, "I'm just happy you were not hurt or kidnapped."

Jane broke down and started to cry. Jane admitted she sent what she thought was a boy name Frank a lot of embarrassing images of her on the computer. The images were of her in various stages of dress and undress. Her friend took many of the photos and they both posted the images online. I had reason to believe the two girls were telling me the truth.

Jane's mother arrived at the police station and I explained to her that her daughter Jane made a mistake and that her daughter needed help right now and not a lecture. Jane's mother agreed that a lecture right now would not benefit Jane or her school friend so she decided to work with me to help Jane.

With her mother present I let Jane talk at her own pace and her statement was very sad. Jane and her school friend admitted to breaking a lot of rules set by their parents as they gave out a lot of personal information over the Internet because they were not thinking about security at the time. Jane just wanted to make a lot of friends online.

After collecting a six-page statement from Jane and a four-page statement from her friend I called the on duty detective Rob and asked for assistance in my investigation.

Investigator Rob read Jane's statement and he taped part of her statement to assist him in his part of the investigation. Rob and I agreed we had enough information to probably get a search warrant and search Richard's house.

Richard slowly manipulated Jane and it appeared that he had a lot of experience and knew how to get his way with young victims. Rob and I just knew that there were other victims on his home computer.

I gave Jane and her mother information to seek a victim's counselor so that she could get help in dealing with being manipulated by Richard.

Richard was read his Miranda rights a second time and he refused to answer questions. Richard was transported to Santa Rita Jail while Rob called the on call duty judge to obtain a search warrant for Richard's home. I typed out my affidavit for the search warrant.

Rob and I drove over to the on call judge's home and we sat in his kitchen as he prepared to read my affidavit and petitions for a search warrant. Just like we were in court, I was sworn in before the judge read my affidavit. The judge took his time and he jotted down notes as he read my affidavit. When he was done reading he said, "good job. It was good you were on duty to help this little girl."

The on call duty judge agreed with my affidavit and petition that we had probable cause to search Richards home and collect any computers, computer files, CD's, printed materials and indicia inside the house.

Rob and I planned to execute the search warrant early the next morning before Richard was able to call someone to go to his home and delete his computer files. Time was important to collect possible evidence.

Investigator Rob and I left the police station early that morning to execute our search warrant. We drove to an exclusive neighborhood in Fremont and located Richards home. His home was on a high hill and had a sweeping view of the bay.

It was a beautiful large home with five bedrooms, three full bathrooms, a gourmet kitchen and a three-car garage. His front door was a beautiful heavy and expensive looking large 60"x80" solid Mahogany double wooden door.

We rang the front door bell twice but there was no answer. We banged on the door twice with no answer.

We yelled out, "Police search warrant, we demand entry" each time with no answer. The house appeared to be unoccupied.

I walked over to my patrol car trunk and took out the international key. The international key is a 60-pound solid metal battering ram that is used by the SWAT team to force entry into a house. It was going to be a treat to take the international key to ram that expensive looking wooden double door.

Rob and I both grabbed a handle on the international key and we took a running start to ram the expensive looking wooden double door. With a little force we were able to open the door. It split into a lot of expensive looking wooden pieces.

The international key worked and we were in the front foyer of the house. We made the police announcement again saying "Hello, Police, search warrant, we are making entry." With no answer we walked into the house.

We quickly searched the house by going room to room and we did not find anyone inside. As we stood in the front foyer of the house an unknown woman drove up and parked in front of the house. She quickly got out and ran to the front door.

She immediately yelled out, "Why did you break down my brother's door?" Rob walked over to her and gave her a copy of our search warrant. She stood in the front foyer reading the search warrant asking, "What is this all about?" She identified herself as Sasha and she was in shock to learn that her brother was in jail.

Sasha told us she received a call from her brother after he was booked into Santa Rita county jail asking her to go to his house and open the door. She claimed that was all she knew about what was going on.

Sasha wanted to know "Who will pay for my brother's front door?" I told Sasha that "a special door repair company is waiting for her to call once we were done collecting evidence." (I hope she did not think we were going to pay for the front door-because we don't). Sasha did not find that as being funny and she returned to her car to place a call on her cell phone.

Rob and I were surprised once we were inside the house. We were prepared to collect one or two computers and a few files. Instead we saw four computers in the dining room, four computers in his office, one computer in his bedroom and four computers in his triple garage. In addition to all the computers we located twenty flash drives or thumb drives, thousands of CD's with kids names and photos on the cover.

I looked at Rob and said, "This is bigger than I thought." Rob responded saying, "Yeah, we're going to need help." I called the police station and requested the utility truck respond to our location to help collect all the evidence located inside the house. My patrol car was too small for all the evidence we were about to collect.

Rob and I searched the house and located a lot of evidence against Richard. There was evidence of a lot of child pornography all over the house.

Once the utility truck arrived the three of us put all the computers, CD's and indicia located inside the house, into the truck. Rob and I had a lot of work yet to do.

We saw a lot of sad videos with children as young as three years old, all races and some possibly living in other states and countries.

On Monday morning Rob called the FBI and they drove over to our station right away. With their help and manpower, we were able to collect a lot of evidence of child pornography against Richard.

Because possible victims, both boys and girls, were located in several states and in international countries the FBI had jurisdiction and they took over the case.

Richard and his attorney were briefed by the FBI and the district attorney on the pornography evidence collected at Richard's home. Richard suddenly wanted to make a deal to avoid courts in other countries.

Richard admitted he was a member of a special club of adult men that took and collected pornographic images of nude juveniles from all over the globe. Richard was able to assist the FBI with the names of five members of his special club. Some of the men have positions as executives of large corporations.

Rob and I were done with our case and now it was time for the FBI and US Marshall's to round up all the members of the special pornography club.

It was good to see that the case was going to be helping kids from all over the world. I was not able to tell Jane a lot of information on her case due to it being an ongoing investigation by the FBI.

I did thank her for coming to me and asking for help. I told her she was "my hero" because she did a brave thing by "telling the truth" about what she did. Jane made a mistake but she did the right thing by reporting her mistake and asking for help. Statistics show that many young victims don't tell what happened to them and the suspects continue for years before they are finally discovered and stopped.

Who would have thought that a 15-year-old girl attending a movie with a school friend, after breaking home restriction, would break a big pornography case?

Whenever I saw Jane on campus I would smile at her and give her a little two-finger salute.

That little two-finger salute from our heart was our secret.

Good job Jane.

Chapter Nineteen

A CAR IN THE SWIMMING POOL

I arrived to work at the usual time when emergency dispatchers notified me to meet with the Castro Valley High School principal Joe Frances and report to the campus swimming pool area. The principal wanted to report that a car was in the school's swimming pool as a senior prank.

I drove over to the high school and there it was, in the swimming pool, a late model brown Datsun sedan at the bottom of the pool. As we stood there looking at the car we noticed several students lining up on the sidewalk outside the fence to see the car and take pictures of the car in the pool. Many of them thought it was pretty funny. What a funny senior prank.

I walked over to the north end of the fence and I noticed the entire fence was cut with wire cutters and once the fenced was breached the Datsun was pushed into the swimming pool.

Joe arranged for a large construction crane and a diver to retrieve the car while school maintenance workers waited. They were prepared to drain the swimming pool and clean the used oil and fluids that had leaked from the car.

As the crane lifted the car out of the pool the local press arrived (I guess it was a slow news day because I did not call them) to take pictures and get a "news scoop" on the senior prank.

Once the car was secured on the back of a tow truck I was able to get the VIN (vehicle identification number) off the vehicle to investigate the owner of the car.

I drove back to the police station and began the computer search to assist in my investigation. I learned the Datsun was sold and registered to a man in Chula Vista, California six years before it ended up in the school swimming pool. I also learned the vehicle was in an accident and was sold as scrap by the local insurance company. The scrap car was sold at an auto auction and shipped to the bay area by another scrap dealer for parts. The car was sold at another auto auction in the Bay Area and the sale was made to a male buyer in a cash transaction. The identification of the buyer could not be confirmed due to the cash transaction for a non-drivable car. The car was towed off the auction lot.

I checked the computer and learned the car was due for a private property tow as the car was considered abandoned in the parking lot at the Castro Valley Miniature Golf course. One day before the car was due to be towed the car disappeared from the property.

I met with the golf course manager to collect a list of employees that saw the abandoned car in the parking lot. On the list were several high school students that showed an interest in the car at the bottom of the swimming pool the day it was discovered.

I also learned the abandoned car was marked for a tow again about two blocks from the miniature golf course. I checked with neighbors and learned two or three juveniles were seen pushing the car down the street late one night.

A week later I met with the principal to give him an update on my investigation. Mr. Frances shared with me that he had several tips from students and parents on who may be responsible for pushing the abandoned car in the school's swimming pool.

We compared names and three names kept showing up on our list as persons of interest. The three boys were all seniors and at an administrator's staff meeting, it was determined that the three boys would be watched closely. The school year was about to end and we were running out of time to close the case.

The next day Mr. Frances received another call about the car in the school swimming pool. The caller was a parent that wanted to report the car incident was recorded and several students were over at her house to view the evidence. The parent gave the names of the students at her house and the same three persons of interest were there. I was getting close.

A check on the three suspects revealed their parents were prominent members of the community and one parent was a practicing attorney. The parents were very active with the school district and business owners in the community. I briefed my patrol command staff and the school superintendent so they could prepare for the negative press and community fallout.

That afternoon I was talking to the school secretary and I told her that I was getting close to making an arrest in the swimming pool case. I told her that I planned on making the arrest on graduation day so that I could make the newspapers like they made the newspapers the day the crane removed the car from the swimming pool. I told her that the students even made a video of the incident and I planned to collect the video as evidence.

Suddenly we both looked at the doorway and saw two female students standing there listening to our conversation. They asked a quick question and left in a hurry. That's when the school rumor mill went into full effect because the girls knew the suspects.

The next day I had a concerned parent that wanted to speak with me in private. I escorted him to my office and the parent wanted information from me about my pending swimming pool case.

The parent identified himself and his son was on my person of interest list. The parents wanted to know if I planned on making an arrest on graduation day. The parent had family coming in from out of town and he was concerned the arrest would make the graduation ceremony a sad event for many families. I told the parent that I could not comment on any pending investigation and that the other parents would have to wait to see the outcome.

He became frustrated with me because he kept asking if I planned on making any arrest on graduation day. When he left my office he was angry but I knew I had the right student's responsible for the vandalism to the school pool.

The next morning, I received a happy call from the school superintendent and the principal Francis. They were happy to report they received a large donation from three parents that wanted to cover the cost of the vandalism of the school swimming pool. By collecting the large donation, the school district wanted to drop the investigation and drop the criminal complaint.

It was just in the nick of time because the next day was graduation day. During the graduation ceremony I stood on a large hill (like I did every year at graduation) overlooking the senior class gathering before the ceremony and I pointed at the graduation seniors. I did it just to make them nervous.

In the end the investigation went well, the school won and I felt I won.

Chapter Twenty

NOT SO INNOCENT

It was the beginning of a new school year in Castro Valley and the beginning of a new school district for a student being transferred in from another state. Jack was that new 9th grade student being transferred to his new school from another state.

Being a new student meant that no one knows who you are, where you have been, what good (or bad) you have done and what you can do. You are a total stranger to everyone at your new school. Jack thought how do I start my reputation at my new school?

That was a tough decision Jack had to make on the first day at his new school. Will I be a nice quiet guy or a real rough and tough guy? Jack decided to be a rough and tough street gangster type guy. (That was his first mistake).

When curious students approached him, Jack tried to set the tone my telling them that he was from a tough school in Los Angeles that was in the middle of gang territory. Jack even said his cousins and friends were drug dealing gang members and they protected him at his old school. None of the information was true.

The true story was he and his mother lived in Nevada and she remarried a man that lived in California. Jack's new stepfather worked as a police officer in the San Francisco Bay Area.

Because Jack told of this gangster lifestyle Jack had to now walk the walk and talk the talk because he probably felt that he was going to be challenged by the schools' tough guys at any time. Jack would walk the halls and go to class with an angry scowl on his face constantly. It was a good acting job.

It didn't take long but the school tough guys decided to ask Jack to join their group because they thought he could intimidate students easier with a reputation of living in the tough gang turf of Los Angeles County. Jack made friends with the wrong group of students.

It didn't take long but now Jack was cutting school, extorting money from students, stealing from students, intimidating students and getting into trouble with his fellow students and teachers. That negative behavior by Jack and his new friends came to the attention of his school administrators. The administrators were quick to suspend them all for things they could prove happening at school.

Jack's mother did not understand what was happening with her son. When she asked him to explain his school suspension Jack said that the school administrators were making things up because they were out to get him kicked out of school.

Since I was the assigned School Resource Officer for the school district, I had several negative encounters with Jack and his friends in the neighborhood when I caught Jack vandalizing personal property during the school lunch breaks. Jack explained our negative encounters by telling his mother that I was part of the conspiracy against him just like the school administrators. Jack's mother bought his claims.

Every time Jack was involved in a violation of the school code of conduct or the school's disciplinary code and facing possible school suspension, Jack's mother came to the school ready for war, accusing everyone of conspiring against her son. According to her, we were all guilty of denying her son a good education.

On one occasion, I met Jack's stepfather, the police officer, and in a private conversation I told him that his stepson Jack was involved in a lot of suspected school extortions and thefts but none of the students wanted to come forward because of the fear of revenge and retaliation because of his tough street gang reputation. I told him about the things students told me in confidence and the stories Jack told students about his reputation.

Jack's stepfather confirmed that none of the stories Jack told other students were true and that neither Jack or his cousins were ever members of any LA street gang. Jack's stepfather said he would talk to his new wife and his stepson Jack but she was very protective of Jack and was not easy to convince. His complaint about their strained marriage was she wanted to be "Jack's friend and not his parent".

When Jack returned to school I saw no change in Jack or his choice of friends. Things did not change and were back to the beginning. It was a long school year.

For the next school year Jack was sent to Redwood Continuation High School because his grades suffered due to all the school cuts and school suspensions. The purpose was to give Jack a new start and pick up extra credits and improve his grade point average.

Jack's new principal at the continuation school was an experienced principal and in his first interview with Jack he was of the opinion that Jack did not want to start over on a new campus.

Jack did not take advantage of his new school and he continued to behave badly. Jack continued to break the school code of conduct and he was suspended many times. Like before Jack's mother would come on campus ready to wage all war against all the people that were out to get her son and denying him of a good education. According to her we were all guilty of conspiracy against Jack.

Then one day a new student was transferred to Redwood Continuation High School from Los Angeles and he met Jack on campus. The new student confronted Jack on his claim of being a LA gang member. The new student being transferred in from LA was a real gang member. Jack tried to bluff the new student but that did not work. The two boys began to fight and Jack lost out big time. Jack forgot he had a knife in his pocket and the principal found the knife when the fight was over.

Jack was suspended from school with a recommendation for an expulsion from school because he was in possession of a knife at school during the fight. Jack's mother was so angry at the school district that she almost needed medication to calm down.

Jack was found guilty by the school board and he was not allowed to attend any school in the school district. Jack had to enroll in another school.

Like before he entered a new school, in a new city, and like before he told students that he was from Los Angeles and a member of a drug dealing street gang. The only part that was true now was that Jack had become a low-level school drug dealer and he kept that a secret from his mother, like all the other secrets he kept from her.

It was a struggle for Jack but he finally graduated from a continuation high school in another city. One day I was at a school meeting located in the city where Jack was a student and I met the School Resource Officer from that school district.

I learned in that school meeting that Jack's mother had the same claim by accusing the school administrators with picking on her son and they all conspired to deny him a good education. The same old excuse I've heard her use to explain Jack's criminal activities and negative behavior. We were all guilty of conspiring against Jack according to her.

Several months after Jack's eighteenth birthday a neighbor contacted Jack's stepfather, the police officer. The neighbor saw Jack breaking into another neighbors home while that neighbor was at work. The neighbor informed him of seeing Jack burglarizing the house.

Jack's stepfather immediately confronted Jack when he arrived home from work and he located the neighbors' stolen property in Jack's room. Jack's stepfather made Jack move out because he was not only a thief but also a drug dealer and a liar about breaking into the neighbor's house.

The stepfather informed his wife and Jack's mother about all the stolen property and that Jack was a daytime home burglar. The family fights led to the stepfather calling the police. Jack was arrested and sent to Santa Rita County Jail. Jack's mother wanted to bail her son out of jail but the stepfather refused to bail Jack out and he refused to drop illegal drug possession charges against his stepson Jack.

Jack told his mother that the illegal drugs were not his and that he did not know the neighbor's property was stolen and that he was just holding all the things located in his room for a friend.

Jack's mother accused her new husband of conspiring against Jack (like all the others) and for not helping Jack succeed in going to college or help finding him a good paying job. I think everyone heard that excuse before.

Jack spent several weeks in jail and was released on probation for burglary and illegal drug possession. Jack did move out of his stepfather's house and he lived in an apartment near their home. Jack's mother helped Jack with his monthly rent and she bought him food and clothes when he asked her for help.

Neighbors living in Jack's apartment complex were cautious around Jack because he told them about his police record and his LA drug gang dealing activities.His neighbors were wise to stay away from him and I think that was what Jack was trying to accomplish. You can sell a lot of stolen property and a lot of illegal drugs if no one wants to witness illegal activities next door. That "No Snitching" street gang attitude can really bring down a neighborhood and that prison or jail attitude can make the neighborhood a dangerous place to live.

That was not Jack's first mistake. Jack did not know that cousins Lew and Tommy sold drugs on his block and Jack did not expect them to confront him on his illegal drug sales business. After all, everyone knew Jack was a hardcore LA gang member with cousins that would drive all the way up North to back him up.

The two cousins stopped by to warn Jack as they were the real drug dealers on the block and they did not want Jack to hurt their drug business. Jack did not take the death warning from two real hard-core drug-dealing thugs as a serious threat. (Another mistake).

A couple of days later Jack committed another daytime burglary and he sold the stolen property from his apartment. To make things worse for Jack he learned where the two cousins lived and he burglarized their house and stole their illegal drugs. Drug dealers don't call the police to report their illegal drugs were stolen. (Drug dealers have a different illegal stolen drug recovery system).

The two cousins asked around the neighborhood and they learned that Jack broke into their home and that Jack stole their illegal drugs. Now we have two angry drug dealers out of business.

The two cousins went over to Jack's apartment and accused Jack of the theft. That led to Jack pulling out a knife from his pocket. Jack flashed the knife in an attempt to scare the two cousins off and possibly defend himself.(How many mistakes can one person make?)

Jack's scare tactic didn't work because one cousin was able to take the knife away from Jack and Jack was stabbed with his own knife. As Jack was lying on the floor bleeding the two cousins searched the apartment and they found their illegal drugs. When they located their illegal drugs they simply stepped over Jack's body and left the apartment.

Jack was found on the floor by a neighbor that just happened to hear him calling for help. The neighbor was coming home from the local grocery store when he came upon the crime scene. 911 was called and the police and emergency personnel responded.

Paramedics tried to help Jack but by the time Jack arrived at the local hospital trauma room it was too late. Jack did not survive his knife wounds.

The two cousins immediately left town to establish an alibi and neighbors questioned by police investigators claimed they did not hear or see anything. The jailhouse or prisons yard "no snitch" policy was in action. No one wanted to cooperate with the police investigations regarding a murder. The bad guys are the minority in our country and the good guys are the majority. The good guys should speak up and tell the truth and make the bad guys look over their shoulders.

Several years after Jack's murder another drug dealer offered information on Jack's murder in order to make a deal for his own freedom. The drug dealer spoke with police investigators and after several additional years, enough evidence was collected to arrest the two cousins for the murder of Jack.

Could this murder have been avoided if Jack would only tell the truth and start fresh in his new school? Could this crime have been avoided if Jack would just follow the school rules? If Jack had told his mother the truth about what was really happening at school maybe his future would have been different. His mother was his biggest advocate and he fooled her with his lies.

Jack made a lot of mistakes in his short life like claiming to be a local gang member and drug dealer. Accusing teachers and school administrators of trying to frame him and conspiring to make him fail in school. Accusing law enforcement, even his stepfather of being corrupt and setting him up for arrest and incarceration.

Jack had a lot of other people to blame for his failures and I was hoping to be wrong but in one private conversation with his mother I remember telling her she "was not doing him justice for not listening to his teachers and school administrators that really wanted to help Jack receive an education. "It is tragic that she did not listen to others about her son."

It is not always a good feeling to be right.

Chapter Twenty-One

THE FELONY PIZZA

A female student, a school administrator with Castro Valley High School and a guidance counselor met with me in my officer at school regarding a serious crime committed on a student while off campus. The matter was very personal and I could see the female student, that I will name Jane Doe, (Her real name protected by state law under Penal code 293)was very upset.

I decided to let the young lady take her time in telling me her story. The female student knew her mother was on her way to school because the school administrator called the mom at work and requested she come to school immediately because her daughter needed her.

I gave her a bottle of water and with the help of the school administrator and counselor the story came out. The 16-year-old student wanted to report she was drugged and raped.

Jane admitted over the past weekend she broke curfew and snuck out of her room late one night to meet an older boy named Carlos.

Carlos knew of a party and he drove Jane to the party for a night of fun. Carlos borrowed his dad's car and they stopped and picked up another two boys that wanted to go to the same party.

While at the party Jane said she was given a lot of alcohol and weed (marijuana) by Carlos to get her in the mood to party. Carlos also gave her an unknown pill to help her relax. Soon Jane began to feel light headed. Carlos suggested Jane should lie down and pace herself. Carlos walked Jane to a bedroom located in the rear area of the house and before she knew it she passed out on the bed.

She woke up to find all her clothing was removed and Carlos was on top of her. Jane told Carlos to stop but he did not stop. Jane could not remember all the details but she thought she passed out again. (The pill Jane described was possibly Rohypnol aka the date rape drug).

Several hours later Jane was able to wake up and she quickly put on her clothing and left the party with another girl she knew from school. Jane had partial memory of what occurred at the party.

Jane told me the next morning she showered and washed her clothing because she was embarrassed, she felt dirty and ashamed of what occurred to her. Jane just wanted to forget about everything that happened.

A couple of friends from school learned about what Carlos did to Jane and they convinced her to report the rape and to get emotional help. Soon Jane's mother arrived and now Jane could start receiving emotional help and support.

Jane was really scared and embarrassed and she wanted me to explain what occurred with her and the reason why Jane's mother was called to school for this special conference.

I asked Jane what was Carlos last name and where did he go to school. Jane was unable to help with that information as she met Carlos at the local mall. Jane said one of her school friends might know more information about Carlos as the school friend met Carlos at the mall first.

Jane did not know the other two boys Carlos picked up and she did not recall the house or the neighborhood, as it was late at night. Jane believes she was in the City of Hayward.

The administrator called Jane's friend to her office but the school friend did not know much about Carlos other than Carlos was about 19 years old and may have once attended school in

Hayward.

I suggested Jane be taken to her family doctor for a physical due to her not being sure whether or not Carlos wore a condom.

The school counselor arranged for Jane to receive rape counseling as well as family counseling to support Jane and her mother.

I left the school and drove to Hayward High School to collect possible information of a former student known only as Carlos. The school administrators in Hayward were very helpful and they gave me three photos of former students with the first name of Carlos.

I placed the photos in a special envelope to construct a photo lineup. The next day I allowed Jane to see the photos and she identified one of the photos as the man she knew as Carlos.

Now I had a confirmed suspect with a last name.

My computer search revealed Carlos had an outstanding warrant for his arrest. The warrant was for eating on a BART train. (Crooks just don't follow any rules)

The search was on for my suspect Carlos that had to have pizza, even on the BART train.

I went to his last known address but I learned that Carlos and his father Carlos Sr. moved away over a year ago. The old landlord had no forwarding address.

Before leaving the apartment complex I asked neighbors if they knew Carlos and if they knew where he lived. I even asked if they had a telephone number for Carlos or his father Carlos Sr. No luck.

As I returned to my patrol car several kids on bicycles, around 6 or 7 years old rode up to me and wanted to know why I was there.

I asked them if they knew Carlos and one little girl said, "Yeah, Carlos used to live over there and he ordered a pizza everyday."(I'm on the right track with the right kids. That is called a clue in law enforcement).

I told her pizza was not good everyday and she replied, "Yeah, my mom won't let me eat pizza everyday but Carlos ate pizza every day. My mom said Carlos is not her child but I'm her child and I can't eat pizza everyday." I asked the kids if they knew where Carlos moved to and one little boy replied, "I see him walking on Western Blvd. all the time but my mom said not to talk to him." (Western Blvd was two blocks away and another clue)

The kids were a big help and I gave the kids police stickers for their bikes and backpacks and I left the apartment complex to drive down Western Blvd.

As I drove down Western Blvd. I saw a pizza delivery driver looking for an address. Could it be Carlos ordered another pizza?

I stuck my hand out of the patrol car window and flagged down the pizza driver. I asked the curious driver if the pizza he was delivering was for Carlos. The driver looked at the order form and saw it was for Carlos. The driver confirmed he was delivering a pizza for Carlos and I said, "Good, what's his address?" The curious driver gave me the address listed on the delivery slip.

I told the driver "Good, it will be good to see Carlos so let's deliver his pizza, but let's make it a surprise." A few blocks later the pizza driver pulled to the curb and pulled the pizza out of the special bag to keep the pizza warm. The driver still had a curious look on his face.

I told the driver that I would wait until he was paid for the pizza so that I could surprise Carlos, but just not to tell Carlos that I waiting to surprise him.

The driver would look at me standing at the corner of the building as Carlos opened the front door and paid for his pizza. I'm sure the pizza driver was very curious as to what I was doing.

The driver was paid and Carlos closed the front door. The driver walked past me and I said, "Thanks, Carlos is going to be so surprised to see me."

I walked to the front door and knocked. Carlos answered the front door and I introduced myself.

I said, "Hello Carlos, I'm Officer Gill and you are under arrest for an outstanding warrant." Carlos was in shock for a minute and I quickly placed him in handcuffs. He objected saying, "I just ordered a pizza and I'm hungry, can you come back?" I said, "No, but we can take your pizza to go."

I walked to the kitchen and I closed the pizza box and escorted Carlos and his pizza to my patrol car. I placed a handcuffed Carlos in the back seat of my patrol car and I placed his pizza in his lap.

When we arrived at the police station a couple of officers made the comment, "What did this kid do, cheated on the pepperoni count when he made the pizza?" I responded saying, "No, but this is the last honest pizza so I'm guaranteed a true confession."

Carlos and I passed a soda vending machine in the hallway of the police station and I bought him and I each a can of soda. I escorted Carlos to a private office for his interview and I informed Carlos that he was under investigation for Penal Code section 261.5-Unlawful sex with under age 18-year-old female and 261(3) Rape Using an Intoxicating Substance. I read Carlos his Miranda Rights and Carlos acknowledged his rights and the interview began.

Carlos could not wait to eat his pizza so he began eating as I interviewed him. My questions began with his personal information for his arrest form.

As Carlos continued to eat pizza I asked him if he recalled a girl named Jane. Carlos responded saying, "Oh yeah, that girl was a real bow-wow, she was short and fat and she should pay me for taking her out."

I asked Carlos if he knew that she was only 16 years old and he responded saying, "I don't care, if she pays she can stay." Carlos had a real hate attitude against women.

As he continued eating pizza Carlos began to brag about all the girls he took out. Carlos admitted he tricked and drugged girls of all ages and races.

Carlos told me he would pick up a lot of young girls at the local mall. Carlos would focus on girls that were a little heavy and plain looking. Some of the girls appeared to have low self-esteem and he looked for that type of young girl. He felt they enjoyed the attention and he was not concerned that they would turn him in. He was pretty proud of himself. I just let him eat and talk.

It took an entire large pizza but Carlos admitted to tricking and drugging Jane with Rohypnol the night of the party. At the end of his confession I had four additional young schoolgirl victims to contact.

I was amazed that Carlos remembered all the young girls' names and the schools they attended. Carlos said, "Even the bow wows would be happy to see him again." Carlos was proud of his accomplishments and he failed to recognize that what he was doing was wrong.

I transported Carlos to Santa Rita jail after receiving his five-page written confession. As I was leaving Carlos in the jail booking area I told him "Good luck and I hope you survive jail because some inmates hate child rapists and they also do not serve pizza everyday here."

Carlos had a confused look on his face and he may not have understood the parting comment I made to him but I have an idea that he understands my parting comment now.

I was happy to get that sick pedophile off the streets and I hope the pizza industry could survive with him serving prison time for now.

Another five cases solved by the SRO.

Chapter Twenty-Two

ONE-DAY AMNESTY

I was on patrol around Castro Valley High School before the morning break time (around 10:00) when I noticed a male student walking across the student parking lot. As I drew closer to him he happened to notice my patrol car approaching him. He immediately ran off campus. (That's called a clue that he was possibly cutting school).

I followed him in my patrol car and I let him run several blocks until he was nice and tired. He was wearing a heavy looking backpack so I assumed his running would end quickly.

My plan worked because he did stop running and he waited for me to pull over to the shoulder of the road. I pulled over and I got out of the patrol car to talk to him.

I asked him "Why are you cutting school today young man?" His reply was, he did not feel good and that he would have his mother call the school to excuse his absence. I asked the student his name and he identified himself as "Danny." I reminded Danny that if he felt ill at school he had to see the school nurse first and that the school nurse would contact his mother before he could officially leave campus.

Danny said, "Oh yeah, I forgot to do that." I replied, "Well Danny I just watched you run with a heavy backpack on and you did not appear to be that sick."

Danny said, "I was feeling good then so I just started to run." "Well Danny you are in luck today because I just happen to be driving back to your school, and I'll just give you a ride back to school."

I opened the rear door to my patrol car and I asked Danny to get in. Before I would allow any person to get into my patrol car I would usually search them. Police officers have been known to die for not searching subjects riding in the rear of a police car. I modified the practice by asking students to pull up their baggy pants pockets and shake them. If the student had an illegal weapon on his or her person the clothing shaking would make the weapon fall. All was good for 16-year-old Danny.

The backpack was a different story. I would never allow a backpack to travel in the rear seat area. The backpack would either be placed in the front seat or the trunk. First I would search the backpack for weapons as well. You would be surprised to find what was in Danny's backpack.

National crime statistics show that one out of every seven students is armed with a knife at school. Both boys and girls take knives to school. The same statistics show that the student armed with a knife becomes a victim of the same knife.

As Danny sat in the back seat of the patrol car I asked him if he had a weapon in his backpack. Danny gave me a nervous, "No." I then said, "Well, let's see if you are telling the truth."

I found miscellaneous school supplies, books, tablets, pens and pencils and a curious binder with graffiti on the cover.

At the bottom of the backpack I found a 6" locking blade pocketknife. I immediately said, "Danny you lied to me, you have a knife." Danny replied "Oh yeah, I forgot I had that knife."

I went back to the curious binder and began looking closer at the graffiti on the cover. Every Monday I would drive around town, mainly behind stores on service roads, and I took photo's of illegal graffiti on buildings and private property. When I opened the binder I got a real surprise. It was full of graffiti drawings and photos.

Graffiti artist call this kind of book a "Piece book". That is street slang or street jargon for masterpiece book. Graffiti artist would show off their illegal art with other street graffiti artists. They would compare their illegal artwork amongst themselves. The street slang is also called a "brag book". They took a lot of pride in their illegal art.

I said, "Danny your problems just keep getting bigger and bigger because according to your piece book you are a street artist". Danny asked, "Are you going to tell my mother?" My reply was "Let's go to the police station to talk about your problems." I informed Danny he was being detained for possible felony vandalism under California Penal Code 594.

I transported Danny to the police station and I contacted his assistant principal Mr. White. I informed Mr. White that I stopped Danny off campus and I located a pocketknife and a graffiti book in his possession. I asked Mr. White to contact Danny's mother Julie at work and inform her of her son's current location. Julie worked for the school district, which was why he was concerned that I would tell his mother.

I walked over to a soda vending machine and another vending machine for a pack of cookies and Danny and I sat together to discuss his problems. I read Danny his Miranda rights and he was very talkative for a kid being in a lot of trouble.

Danny claimed he forgot he had the pocketknife in his backpack and as far as the graffiti binder he admitted he was a graffiti artist. Danny began to brag about all the illegal art he was responsible for.

I asked Danny if he was part of a graffiti crew and he admitted he was a member of a crew. As Danny continued to talk I asked him to name his graffiti crew. Danny said his crew had three other members but he refused to name them.

I informed Danny I could get his friends names from Mr. White or campus supervisors Joyce, Doris or even his mother since she worked for the school district. That comment must have sent a chill down his back because he said, "Ok, Ok, but you can't tell them I gave you their names".

Danny gave me the names of Andrew, Eric and Ben. Once that information was out Danny went on to give me his friends' tagger monikers (graffiti names).

Danny told me that he and his friends would sneak out late at night to "tag up the town". They would steal their parent's cars late at night and one would act as a lookout while the other three would spray paint their graffiti on buildings. They would stay out for hours and they would not return home until they all got a chance to put their tag on a building. Danny said that he and his friends were very competitive and they all wanted to do as much graffiti as they could.

Danny was very helpful now and he gave me a six-page written statement. Danny even drew his and their tag on the statement form.

When Danny was through confessing I realized the victims were Cal Trans, BART, East Bay Water District, Union Pacific Railroad, AC transit public transportation, three shopping centers, two school districts and several private property owners.

Danny was very helpful and the graffiti damage was estimated at over $55,000. That is called a felony vandalism case and all because a kid was cutting school.

I told Danny I would try to get him community service amnesty for his statement and assistance but I may not be able to get community service or amnesty for his friends. I asked Danny to "let's keep his confession and statement between us for now." Danny thought that was a good idea. It was now official; Danny and I had a secret confession.

I transported Danny back to the high school and as I drove towards his school it was lunch period with many students walking around campus.

That is when Andrew, Eric and Ben saw their friend and fellow tagger Danny getting out of my patrol car. I saw them whisper something to each other as we walked to the assistant principal's office. They looked nervous.

I briefed Mr. White on Danny's confession and he was told to wait in the office until his mother arrived. Danny was now very nervous.

I had to leave the school for another call for service but at the end of the school day I was once again in the area of the high school patrolling the area.

As I traveled through the student parking lot my cell phone rang. It was the assistant principal's secretary Marjory. Marjory wanted to know if I planned on returning to the assistant principal's office.

I told her I could if she needed me there right away. Marjory said, "There are three boys here in the office waiting for you and they want some kind of secret confession deal?" I told Marjory that I was on my way to the office.

When I walked into the assistant principal's office I saw Andrew, Eric and Ben sitting on a bench. Andrew quickly stood up and said, "We want the same secret deal you gave Danny."

I asked them how did they learn about the secret deal and they said Danny's mother told their mothers that Danny made a secret confession deal about the graffiti. Andrew, Eric and Ben said in unison, "We want the same secret deal." So much for keeping his confession a secret from his friends.

I escorted the three boys to my office on campus and I read them all their Miranda right. They told me they knew their rights because they saw it on TV.

I handed each boy a statement form and they quickly wrote down their confessions. Every now and then I would stop the boys and ask them to read part of the confession aloud. When a confession was read out aloud one boy would correct the other admitting to additional vandalism they forgot about. I guess they wanted their confessions to be correct.

When it was all over each boy wrote out a five to six-page confession admitting to vandalizing a lot of public and private property. Each boy even drew his tags on the statement form.

I called their parents and released the boys with a Notice to Appear before juvenile youth court.

I told each parent and each boy that I would recommend community service for graffiti cleanup and removal but I could not guarantee every victim wanted community service.

I told them with some public service agencies community service may not be allowed due to child labor laws, local labor unions, state workers compensation and insurance restrictions. They all understood and wanted to take their chances with juvenile youth court.

It was another big case solved by the SRO who just stopped a student for cutting school for the day.

Chapter Twenty-Three

MEET ME AT THE FLAGPOLE

On three separate occasions, in the City of Dublin, I learned of three students were struck by cars with mixed results. Two were not seriously injured, just shaken up a little and one student received a broken leg.

I decided to enforce state bicycle helmet laws that required all juveniles under 18 years old to wear a DOT (Department of Transportation) approved safety helmet. I spoke with all the school principals and asked them to make an announcement that I was going to enforce this law to help students get home safe.

Later that week I had a student named Gordon that refused to wear his bicycle helmet. Fourteen-year-old Gordon told me he was a good bicycle rider and that wearing a helmet was "not cool".

I stopped him on three occasions and issued him three bicycle helmet tickets but he was a pretty stubborn kid that refused to wear an un-cool helmet.

Gordon's parents would just pay his court fine because they could not get him to wear his helmet either.

Later on that month I had a call about a student struck by a car just before ending my shift. I was in the staff locker room changing into my civilian clothing and preparing to go home when I overheard the police radio broadcast.

The next day I spoke with a traffic officer and I asked him about the school kid struck by a car as I was leaving the police

171

station and on my way home. The traffic officer said the accident was with a LOL (Little Old Lady) and a kid named Gordon.

I asked how serious was the accident and was the student all right? The traffic officer told me Gordon was rushed to the trauma hospital with a serious head injury. The last the traffic officer heard of Gordon was that Gordon was in critical condition and he was on life support in the ICU (Intensive Care Unit) at the hospital.

The traffic officer told me it was not the LOL's fault as Gordon rode his bicycle through a very busy traffic intersection against the traffic light and directly in front of the LOL. The LOL could not react in time as at the same time she was temporarily blinded by the sun due to the sun setting. Many drivers and pedestrians at the intersection witnessed the accident.

As I reported to duty I received a call on my cell phone. The caller was the assistant superintendent Dr. Dave Malcolm of the school district.

Dr. Malcolm was calling on behalf of the school superintendent and a school board member. They were wondering if I heard about the student injured by a car on his way home from school and if I had an update on the student's condition.

I drove over to the school districts office and Dr. Malcolm and I drove over to Eden Medical Hospital in Castro Valley to get an update on Gordon.

I was in luck that day as I ran into a hospital administrator that I knew. I was invited on several occasions to lecture Castro Valley hospital doctors and nurses on current gang activities.

I asked Nancy if Dr. Malcolm and I could get an ICU update on Gordon. Nancy called the unit and spoke with a nurse that worked in that unit. I was in luck again as Gordon's parents were in the unit visiting their son.

The parents were looking for me and they had questions for me regarding the accident. I agreed to meet with them in the visiting room outside the ICU.

When we met I introduced Dr. Malcolm who was representing the school district and Gordon's school principal and myself.

Gordon's parents Kelly and Joseph wanted to thank me for insisting on making Gordon wear his bicycle helmet. They admitted they should have done a better job on supporting my insistence on wearing a helmet and not just pay his court fines.

The parents allowed us to go inside the ICU and see Gordon and speak with his nurse. We stood next to Gordon's hospital bed and I saw bandages around his head, tubes everywhere and blinking and ringing machines that appeared to be helping Gordon breathe. Gordon looked to be in a lot of pain.

When Dr. Malcolm and I returned to the school district's office I decided to go to each school within the district and make an announcement on the school's PA system informing all students that I would start enforcing California Vehicle Code 21212(a)-All persons under 18 years of age are required to wear safety helmets when operating bicycles, skateboards, rollerblades and razor type scooters.

That same day I drove to each school and met with the principal. Each principal allowed me to make my announcement over the school's public address system.

I started with saying, "Hello students, I'm sorry for the class interruption but this is Officer Gill, your School Resource Officer with an important safety announcement". At the end of the school day it was official. All the students attending school that day received their bicycle helmet warning.

At the end of school leaving the high school I caught two students not wearing their bicycle helmets. They heard the warning given over the school PA system that morning. Both students claimed, "They forgot." I did not forget and they were issued citations for violating the helmet law. Since it was first day of enforcement I allowed the students to work off their citation by collecting ten friends with bicycles to meet me on campus at the end of the week with all of them wearing their bicycle helmets. (It was a little peer pressure to teach them all an important lesson).

As the weeks went by I came up with other programs to teach students bicycle safety lessons. I would often allow students the choice to either work off their citation by performing community service at school or community service at a senior center in town.

If they decided to perform community service at school, they had to work with school cafeteria or grounds keepers during their lunch period. If they chose the senior center they had to help clean up the senior center on their Saturday.

At the end of their community service choice I would give the student a new bicycle helmet with the understanding they would not receive a second chance if caught violating the helmet law again.

A couple of weeks later I caught five Wells Middle School boys without their bicycle helmets. They identified themselves for their citations as Tim, Parker, Nolen, Bradley and Jason. They "forgot" their helmets too.

I wanted them to understand the law so each boy was told to write a five to six-page essay on bicycle helmet safety. I told them that I would not accept information just downloaded off the Internet as their essay. They were to include current research listing the reason why the law was written, statistics on bicycle injuries, which lawmaker introduced the law, and how long has the law been on the books.

Each boy was given five days to complete their essay and at the end of five days I would meet with all of them at the end of their school day on their campus. The meeting spot was the school flagpole located in the center of the middle school. They all knew where the flagpole was located.

Each boy agreed and understood their assignment and at the end of their lecture each boy was allowed to walk home with a citation to be worked off.

The day before their essay deadline I happen to see Nolen on the schoolyard. I reminded him that he and his friends were to meet me tomorrow at the flagpole with their completed essay. Nolen said, "We will be there".

The next day I drove to the middle school to meet the boys. I parked my patrol car in the parking lot near the flagpole. I got out and walked on the sidewalk looking for the boys. They were not at the flagpole. Where were the boys?

I could see a group of boys playing in the campus basketball court. The basketball court was approximately 75 yards away. I took a closer look and I could see the boys and I could see their bicycles lying on the ground near them.

They were not at the flagpole like they agreed to be in order to meet with me and turn in their essays. They were playing on campus. (Would you believe a group of boys would play on a school playground?)

I decided to return to my patrol car and maybe wait but at the last minute I decided to drive through the campus parking lot.

As I slowly drove away I saw one boy had spotted me and he was trying to get my attention. He was frantically waving at me. His friends joined in and now they are all yelling out and all were trying to get my attention.

I decided at the last minute to teach them a lesson. I slowly drove towards the main road and from my rear view mirror I could see them, almost in a panic, put on and buckle their helmets and grab their bicycles.

I made a right turn and drove slowly on the main road away from the school. I was watching the boys from my rear view mirror and I could see they were trying to get my attention.

I continued to slowly drive away from the campus and I would glance over to my rear view mirror to see the boys were trying to gain distance and catch me. I continued to slowly drive away at about 15 mph.

After a couple of blocks I glanced in the rear view mirror and I saw the boys had stopped and they decided to walk their bicycles on the sidewalk. They appeared to be in an argument maybe accusing each other of not looking out for my patrol car.

I pulled over to the curb and I engaged a couple of students with friendly conversation. I asked them if they had a good day in school and if they had seen Tim, Parker, Nolen, Bradley or Jason. They all responded saying, "No, they had not seen them."

Once the boys saw I had pulled my patrol car over to the curb the boys jumped back on their bicycles and once again they rode their bicycles towards my patrol car desperately trying to catch me.

I was watching the boys from my rear view mirror and before they drew too close I decided to slowly drive away. They appeared to be in a panic by yelling "Officer Gill, wait, we're here, wait Officer Gill."

I decided to drive two blocks and I made a right turn to drive back to the campus. The boys were right behind me trying to get my attention.

As I slowly drove about 15 mph down the street once again I saw from my rear view mirror the boys stop and rest on the sidewalk.

I again pulled over to the curb and engaged in friendly conversation with students walking home. I asked, "How was school today?" and their reply was the same as the first group. I asked them if they saw Tim, Parker, Nolen, Bradley or Jason. Like the first group they responded with "No."

Like before the boys saw that I had pulled my patrol car over to the curb and again they were back on their bicycles.

I could see the boys from my rear view mirror that they were once again trying to get my attention. When they drew closer I slowly pulled away from the curb and slowly drove about 15 mph towards the school.

I made another right turn and a few hundred feet later I was back on the middle school campus. I slowly drove back to the flagpole and I stopped near the sidewalk. I got out of the patrol car and waited on the sidewalk. I was leaning against the patrol car with my arms crossed.

A few minutes later the five boys were back on campus riding their bicycles towards me. They were yelling, "Officer Gill. We're here, wait, we're here."

They rode up to me and they tried to speak but they were all out of breath. They were trying to say, "Officer Gill, we were here looking for you but you did not see us. We tried to catch up with you and we followed your police car."

I had to hold back my laughter and I said, "Where have you guys been? I've been looking all over for you guys, I drove around the school and I asked other students if they saw you guys but they said that they did not see you."

They said over and over again that they were here looking for me and I said, "I was here at the flagpole looking for you. When I was here at the flagpole I did not see any of you guys. Where were you guys?"

They were still out of breath and they all tried to answer all at once. I just stood there trying not to laugh.

I noticed Jason had a very nervous look on his face because his mother worked for the school district. He had a lot to lose if he could not turn in his essay.

I said, "Jason, I know you and you have always told me the truth, so tell me the whole story, where were you guys?"

Jason said, "We were here at the flagpole waiting when Parker wanted to play basketball. We put our bicycles near the basketball court and we wanted to play until you arrived". Jason went on to say, "Nolen was to look out for you but he started playing with us too. Tim saw you and we tried to get your attention. We followed behind you in your patrol car and we followed you back to the school flagpole."

I reminded them that the deal was to meet at the flagpole but now thanks to Jason I now understood why they were not at the flagpole.

I asked Jason to hand me his essay and I read the essay in front of them. I accepted Jason's essay and I collected his copy of the citation. I told Jason he was officially warned.

I asked who was next and Tim gave me his essay. I read his essay and I accepted his essay. I gave Tim an official warning and I collected his copy of the citation.

Parker went next then Nolen and Bradley were last. I read all of their essays and like the others I officially issued them a warning after collecting their copies of their citations.

They all rode away with their helmets on and happy to receive an official warning for riding a bicycle without a helmet.

A lesson learned, a little exercise performed and another problem solved by the SRO.

Chapter Twenty-Four

THE SECRET GAME

I was just ending my duty shift when I received a cell phone call from Principal Lisa Ross at Castro Valley High School. Lisa said she needed me back on campus right away. Her call sounded urgent so I drove right over to collect information on her call for service.

When I arrived in Principal Ross's office she was with two angry and upset parents. I was told they wanted to report a serious crime against the special education student in the office.

Principal Ross said the parent of the special education student told her of a sensitive crime against her daughter and the mother did not want her daughter's name used in the police report. To comply with California Penal Code 293 the student's real name is confidential and in this story she will be identified as Jane Doe.

The adults in the room were identified as Natalie, mother of a special education student, Ada the aunt of a special education student, special education teacher Heidi and the female special education student Jane Doe.

Natalie said her daughter Jane is 19 years old but has the mental capacity of an eight or ten year girl. Her reading capacity is on a 5th grader reading level and her communication skills are limited.

As she choked back her tears Natalie said her daughter Jane had been sick for several days. Jane was throwing up everyday and she missed her monthly menstrual cycle. Natalie took Jane to her doctor today and after the doctor's examination her doctor informed Natalie that Jane was pregnant.

Teacher Heidi said there are three boys in Jane's class but they were never left alone with Jane. There was only one male teacher and three female teacher aides in addition to the seven students in the special education class.

Jane Doe's aunt Ada said there are no males in their home as Jane's father left over fifteen years ago and she and her sister Natalie did not have male friends that spend the nights at their residence.

All the women wondered how Jane became pregnant because Jane had no boyfriend and Jane did not understand sex. After several attempts to interview Jane I suggested Natalie and Ada take Jane home so that she was comfortable with familiar surroundings.

I decided to use one of my interview techniques to try to interview Jane and get some needed answers. I asked Jane what was her favorite ice cream flavor and I told Natalie and Ada that I would stop by the ice cream store before I met them at their home. All the ladies in the office had a curious look on their faces.

After stopping to get ice cream I began interviewing Jane in her kitchen. As we ate ice cream I asked Jane if a boy at school was friendly to her lately. She said, "No." I asked Jane if she liked playing games and she said, "I like playing chutes and ladders and sometimes the secret game."

I asked Jane how do you play the secret game and she said, "It a secret." I asked, "Jane who taught you how to play the secret game" and she said, "Rodger taught me the secret game but sometimes he hurt me."

Natalie said, "Rodger is our 16-year-old neighbor." I asked Jane "where do you and Rodger play the secret game" and she said everyday in the garage.

180

Ada said there was an old used unattached garage near the rear area of the property. I asked Jane if she and Rodger played the secret game in the old garage and Jane said, "Yes we play the secret game in the garage everyday." I asked Jane if she and Rodger played the secret game after school and she said, "Yeah every day after school."

Natalie said, "Rodger should be home now because school is out." Ada said, "I wonder if Rodger is in the garage now waiting for Jane?" I said, "Well I'll just have to go and check out the old garage."

I left the kitchen and walked out to the old garage located near the rear property line. I noticed the garage door was unlocked and I opened the garage door to find a 16-year-old boy standing inside the garage in his underwear and with his pants off.

The young boy was surprised to see a uniformed police officer standing at the door of what was supposed to be an abandoned garage. I know I was surprised to see a young boy standing inside an abandoned garage in his underwear.

I said, "Rodger, let's put your pants back on and come with me." As the young boy was quickly putting his pants back on he said, "I can explain." I said, "I can't wait to hear your explanation because you got a lot of explaining to do." I informed Rodger that he was being detained for Penal Code 261(1)-Rape of a Mentally Disable Female.

As I walked out of the old garage with Rodger I noticed Natalie and Ada race to the rear kitchen door to yell at Rodger. They were extremely angry and enraged with Rodger. I noticed a very nervous look on his face. When we made it to my parked patrol car I asked Rodger if his parents were at home. It was quite a task to keep Natalie and Ada away from him.

Rodger said his mother did not make it home until around 7:00 pm due to her long work commute and his father lived in Oregon. I told Rodger that I was going to take him to the police station for his own safety. Rodger agreed he was probably much safer at the police station.

To try and calm Natalie and Ada I suggested that they take Jane to her doctor's office and request a test for possible STD. They yelled at Rodger as he sat in my patrol car, "Jane better not have an STD!" in addition to other angry comments.

I wanted to warn Rodger's mother Hazel, about the events with her angry neighbors. When we arrived at the police station I made several attempts to contact his mother but she left her job site early and was probably in commute traffic.

I read Rodger his Miranda rights and he agreed to give me a written statement. I offered to wait for his mother to arrive at the police station but Rodger did not want his mother to hear him admit to having sex with his mentally challenged neighbor.

I decided to tape Rodger's statement in addition to writing it down on the standard statement form. Sometimes suspects have a sudden lapse in memory and forget what they said in written statements and I wanted the court to hear Rodger's own words.

Secondly, I did not want Jane to possibly appear in scary Superior court and be subjected to tough questions by attorneys as she is mentally challenged even though she is 19 years old.

And thirdly, I wanted all involved to understand that I did not threaten, force, coerce or bully a confession from Rodger. The tape recorder was in plain sight on the table between Rodger and myself.

My first question to Rodger was "Tell me all about the secret game you taught Jane."

At first Rodger tried to make light of the secret game question until I informed him that he was looking at possible serious statuary rape charges due to Jane being unable to give consent to have sex. Rodger thought about the charges and he changed his flippant answers.

I learned that Rodger's bedroom overlooked Jane's backyard and he would look at Jane everyday after school, as Jane would often play with a ball or a balloon in the backyard.

Rodger noticed her body was fully developed and he was curious about how much she understood about sex. Rodger came up with a plan to talk with Jane and he decided to play ball with Jane in an attempt to get to know her better. When Rodger went over to meet Jane he was able to check out the abandoned garage.

Suddenly a plan began to develop for Rodger as he found out Jane was naïve, trusting, kind and unable to communicate "no" like all the other girls at his school. To make his plan sound better in his mind, he realized that Jane was 19 years old and she had a fully developed female body.

Rodger admitted he tricked Jane into following him inside the old garage and he started the secret game. The secret game was simply Rodger throwing a small ball to Jane. If Jane missed or dropped the ball she had to kiss Rodger as her penalty. Of course Rodger would either throw the ball too high or too far away so that Jane could not catch the ball.

After a couple of days of just kissing the game rules changed. As a new penalty Jane was to allow Rodger to feel out Jane's breast. When Jane did not object to him feeling her breasts he decided to trick her once again into taking off her clothes.

After several weeks Jane began to trust Rodger so Rodger tricked Jane into having sex as part of the new secret game penalty. We now know Rodger's penalty was arrest because he was having unprotected sex with Jane and now she was pregnant.

At the end of his written statement I asked Rodger if he wanted to change or correct any lines in his statement and I also asked Rodger if everything said was true and correct. Rodger read and signed his statement and I stopped the recording.

I received a telephone call from Rodger's mother Hazel, but it was too late as Natalie and Ada were waiting for her to arrive from work. They were very angry and they gave her full details about Rodger and why Rodger was in custody. That is not a good ending to a long traffic commute.

Natalie and Ada told me later that Jane tested negative for all STD's and that the doctor gave them information and options to consider terminating Jane's pregnancy due to her severe mental incapacity.

I transported Rodger to Juvenile Hall where he was held for 37 days before he appeared in court.

Rodger was found guilty of unlawful sex with a mentally ill female and sent to live with his father in the State of Oregon after serving five years in the California Youth Authority.

This was a very sad case for all involved. No winners and all losers.

Chapter Twenty-Five

TAGGER FOOTBALL

I received a call from school maintenance workers with Dublin Unified School District who discovered graffiti on an elementary school. I drove to their location to collect additional information on their call for service. The maintenance crew wanted to show the graffiti before they painted over the damage.

The graffiti was strange because it was only numbers and girl's names. The graffiti read, "#28 loves Tonya, #72 loves Nicky and #56 loves Anna." As I spoke with the maintenance crew I took photos and I said the numbers might be football players' numbers because that was the only thing that made sense. I immediately drove over to the high school and spoke with the high school football coach.

The coach took a look at the photos and said all the numbers were possibly junior varsity football players and that "#28 is Paul, #72 was Josh and #56 was Kevin." I asked if they had girlfriends and he stated Paul's girlfriend was Tonya, Josh's girlfriend was Nicky and Kevin's girlfriend was Anna. I asked which player was the weak link and he immediately replied, "Paul, because his mother worked for the school district and his dad was a retired police officer. Between the two parents they will make him confess."

Now I have suspects and I drove over to Paul's house to contact his parents. Paul's house was about two blocks from the elementary school with all the graffiti damage. (That may be a law enforcement clue).

I rang the bell and Paul's mother answered the door. She invited me inside her home and asked what I needed. Paul's dad, the retired police officer, was also at home so I was in luck.

I showed Paul's parents the graffiti photos and she said, "You are in luck today because Paul, Josh, and Kevin were in her family room playing video games with their girlfriends Tonya, Nicky and Anna. They were all at her house. Paul's father called all the boys into the dining room to answer questions about the graffiti.

At first all the boys denied any involvement with the graffiti but their parents joined in and began questioning the boys. While the girlfriends looked on and had a nervous look on their faces they knew they were next to answer questions. The retired cop and the school district secretary were hard on the boys and their excuses began to fall apart.

Paul's mother told the boys it was embarrassing to her because she worked for the school district. Paul's dad said he was embarrassed because he was a retired police officer and his son was involved in graffiti vandalism. The boys took a long look at each other and the truth came out.

Paul was the first to admit his involvement. Josh admitted his part followed by Kevin admitting taking part in writing graffiti on the school building. This was the easiest graffiti investigation I ever conducted.

Paul's mother called Josh and Kevin's mothers and they came over to collect their sons. All the parents agreed that the boys should immediately go to the school and help the maintenance workers remove their graffiti. Paul's dad said, "I guarantee all the damage would be taken care of today." He then told the boys to change their clothes because they have a lot of work to do today.

Another juvenile crime solved by good, responsible and involved parents and the SRO.

Chapter Twenty-Six

GOOD JOB MAX

I was on patrol around Castro Valley High School when the campus maintenance worker called me on the cell phone. He wanted to report a large dog on the campus football field. He told me he was not sure if the dog was vicious or not but he wanted me to be aware that students were going to take the campus football field for their PE class in about ten minutes.

I knew all the back roads and alleys to the campus and I was able to drive onto the campus football field. When I arrived I saw a large German Shepard dog having fun on the twenty-yard line area of the football field. I gave a loud whistle and the dog stopped and looked at me. I gave a second loud whistle and the dog ran towards me.

As I stood there I thought to myself, "Oh boy, I hope this is a friendly dog". I guess I will find out in a couple of seconds because he is running towards me.

To my surprise the dog was old and friendly. I gave the dog a pet on his head and I rigorously rubbed around his neck area. I noticed a dog tag around his collar and I read the inscription on the tag. The dog's name was "Max" and his owner lived about six blocks from the school.

Max found the school after walking through a lot of heavy traffic. Max was a lucky dog negotiating through all that heavy traffic to find a nice open field area to play.

I walked over to my patrol car and I opened the rear door.

Max automatically jumped into the rear compartment of my patrol car without a command to do so. I was relieved Max was a well-trained dog.

I was able to leave the football field without any students seeing Max or me. I was on my way to Max's owners house when I was informed of an emergency traffic accident that just occurred less than two blocks from the high school campus.

I responded to the traffic accident to check on injuries. CHP (California Highway Patrol) had jurisdiction on traffic accidents in un-incorporated Castro Valley and I did not expect to be at the traffic accident site for very long.

When I arrived both drivers claimed they were unharmed but both cars did a good job of trading paint and bodywork. One car had a broken front axle and needed a tow truck to remove it from the road. I advised emergency radio dispatchers and I directed traffic until I was relieved by the CHP. Friendly Max was still in the rear compartment of my patrol car.

I directed traffic for about twenty minutes and I was relieved by CHP who investigated the traffic accident. I returned to Max and I decided to return to the school cafeteria to get a bowl of water for Max because it was a warm day.

Before I could return to Max the school lunch bell rang and now students were heading off campus to buy their junk food lunches. I always parked my patrol car near the student parking lot exit to remind student to slow down as they drove off campus. A marked patrol car is always a good speed deterrent.

As the students drove off campus in their cars they all saw Max the dog in the rear compartment of my patrol car. Max would sometimes bark at cars. I guess that is how dogs say hello. All the students were curious as to why I had a big German Sheppard dog in the rear compartment of my patrol car. Their minds were racing about what they saw.

As usual I drove around the campus and I drove to the usual spots where large groups of students ate their lunch. Their minds were racing as well as to why I had a big German Shepard dog in my patrol car.

When the lunch period was about to end I returned to my usual spot on the side of the road near the campus parking lot entry. I did my daily lunch hour routine and students were back on campus.

I drove over to Max's owners house and before I allowed Max to leave my patrol car I walked over to the front door and rang the doorbell. There was no answer so I walked to the side gate and I saw the gate was closed but I also saw two long wooden fence slots lying on the ground. I took a look at the fence and determined that is how Max was able to leave his backyard.

I saw a car parked in the driveway of the next-door neighbor so I walked over and rang the neighbor's doorbell. The neighbor identified herself as Megan and she was a stay-at-home mom with twin sons. I informed Megan why I was there and I asked her if she knew how I could contact her neighbor regarding their dog Max.

Megan said, "Max got out?" and I informed her that I located a couple of missing wooded fence slots and this is how Max was able to run free. Max was able to get to the high school football field until I was able to get him back home. Megan said, "Well Max can just stay in my backyard with my dog because my three-year-old sons love to play with Max."

I walked over to my patrol car and took Max out to enjoy freedom again. Max ran to Megan's backyard after she opened her side fence gate. I saw her twin sons playing with their friend Max. Everyone was happy. I returned to the front door of Max's owner home and I left a business card in the door explaining how I was able to locate Max and return him home.

I was back to my patrol around the high school. Suddenly my cell phone ran and it was Principal Lesley Blackwell. Lesley stated she needed to see me in her office right away because she had to return a telephone call to a school board member immediately.

When I arrived on campus I went straight to Principal Blackwell's office and I asked her what information would she like to know. Leslie told me she received a telephone call from a school board member (it must have been an election year) that wanted to know, "Why did you bring a drug dog on campus today?"

The school board had debated the topic of allowing trained drug detection dogs on the high school campus for months. The school board had not determined if they would allow trained drug detection dogs on the high school campus yet.

Now the rumor around campus was I brought a drug dog on campus to search for illegal drugs. Students leaving campus for the lunch period saw Max in my patrol car and assumed Max was a drug dog. Students called each other on their cell phones with their opinion about Max.

Every area that I patrol - the area park, all the side streets adjacent to the school and the convenience store near the school, students saw Max and during the lunch period and Max caused a lot of student talk.

Principal Blackwell informed me that a student reporter wrote an article about Max the drug dog in the student newspaper. Leslie said we had to do something about the student newspaper article. She called the English teacher and student newspaper editor Libby to her office right away.

As we waited for Libby to arrive Leslie told me her campus supervisors reported students were acting very strange during the lunch period. Many students, both boys and girls suddenly had to rush to the restroom and the sounds of toilets flushing were heard all over the campus. Max made quiet an impact on their behavior.

When Libby arrived we informed her of the true story of Max and that the student newspaper reporter wrote the article of Max based on student rumor only. Libby said it might be too late because the newspaper article is ready for print.

Principal Blackwell asked Libby to have a conversation with the student reporter about reporting the truth and not listening to student rumor. Also the reporter should next time write a newspaper story that has been verified and confirmed before offering it to the student newspaper. Libby said that she guaranteed that the next time she would carefully read every article and not just take the students reporter's word that the article is accurate and correct.

I had a suggestion to solve the school newspaper article that was about to print. I suggested to Libby that since April 1st was only two days away we should just add one line at the end of the newspaper article. I said, "Just add April Fools at the end of the article." We all broke out in laughter.

Principal Blackwell called all the school board members and the school districts' superintendent to update them all on Max.

Another case for the SRO and another problem solved. Ha-HaHa.... April Fools.

Chapter Twenty-Seven

CALLING ALL
BICYCLE VANDALS

It was another Monday morning and after morning patrol muster I would walk to my internal mailbox to collect messages. The daily patrol muster was held to inform the on-coming patrol shift about what occurred on the prior patrol shift. Muster information is very helpful to start the day's shift work.

I walked to my mailbox and I saw a huge police report waiting for me to read. Officer Ashley Clark wrote the police report that was written on her night patrol shift during the weekend. As I began reading the front page of the report I saw it was regarding a felony vandalism (Penal Code 594) that occurred at Wells Middle School.

The report stated the midnight patrol shift received a silent alarm call after the alarm company heard glass breaking with multiple voices and other sounds in the background.

The midnight patrol shift responded to the silent alarm call at the school and the officers were able to detain twenty-one juveniles that were trespassing on the school campus around 12:30 AM Friday night, or if you prefer Saturday morning.

All the juveniles trespassing rode their trail bicycles. The report indicated that each bicycle had long metal pegs on the rear wheels of the bicycles. The boys would grind their bicycle rear wheel pegs on the sides of buildings, playground equipment, benches and anything that appeared to be a challenge to them. The trail bicycles caused a lot of the damage done to the campus.

The report included crime scene photos that were taken of the damage to the school.

I took the police report and drove over to the middle school to meet with the principal. Principal Robert Sheppard was informed of the damage done by the early morning maintenance workers as he arrived to his school campus.

I informed Principal Sheppard that the midnight patrol shift caught twenty-one high school and middle school students over the weekend after the alarm company received a silent alarm. I read the list of boy's names that were detained that morning and he was familiar with many of them as well as their parents. Robert was in shock to hear some of the names as their parents were very active and involved in the school and school district.

As Robert and I sat in his office his telephone began to ring. The callers were parents of the detained students involved in the school vandalism. They were calling to apologize to the principal for their son's actions that night.

When Principal Sheppard ended his telephone calls his secretary June knocked on the door and handed him more telephone messages from parents that wanted to apologize for their sons as well.

Principal Sheppard said, "I don't know what to do because some of these boys are from good families. They made a mistake and yes they have to pay for their mistake so, somehow we have to help them. What can we do to help them?"

I informed Robert that I would contact the juvenile district attorney and ask if the boys can do community service to repay for their vandalism damage. I left saying I will have to come up with a plan to help everyone and the school district.

I returned to the police station and I called the juvenile district attorney and informed him of the huge vandalism case I was just handed that morning. I asked him if it was all right if I came up with a community service project that would satisfy the juvenile court and the school district. His answer was "Do what is necessary to make the victim happy and that will make my office happy.

Now I have to come up with a plan. I started by meeting with Paul, the school district's maintenance director. I asked Paul if the school district would be willing to supply all the paint, paints brushes, rags and everything needed to paint and repair the damage the boys did at the middle school. Paul said, "Yes, if they are willing to repair the damage we are willing to provide the supplies." The first part of my plan was in action.

I met with Principal Sheppard and informed him of my community service project idea. Robert said he was willing to call all the parents and arrange for a meeting for parents and their sons to meet in the school gym after school on Wednesday afternoon. He said, "Yes, I'll start calling parents right now." Part two of my plan in action.

I've never attempted to do a huge community service project like this before so I had to sit down and work on all aspects to make the plan work. On Wednesday I was prepared to tell everyone of the plan.

After school ended that afternoon Principal Sheppard and I walked into the school gym and we met with all the parents and boys that were willing to volunteer in our community service project. I informed every person in the gym that on Saturday stating at 9:00 am we were going to repair and paint all the damage caused by the boys and their bicycles.

I ended by informing the parents that I need at least one parent to be on campus to supervise their son during the repair project. I saw parents looking at each other and looking at their sons during my speech. It didn't take long for a decision because all the parents agreed to have their sons there on campus to perform their community service. Part three of the plan.

I called Paul at the district maintenance office and he agreed to have all the paint and supplies on the middle school campus by Saturday morning. This plan may work.

On Thursday afternoon I received a call from the parent of Kyle. Parents Jim and Kim informed me that his son Kyle would not be at the community service project as promised. Jim said, "I spoke with my neighbor that knows an attorney and he told me that we did not have to volunteer for any community service project, so my son and I will not be there." I answered saying, "Well if that's your decision, good luck because I will be sending your son's case to the juvenile district attorney's office."

Before Jim rudely hung up the telephone he said, "Tomorrow is my day off and I plan to play golf so, I guess we will be seeing you in court."I said to myself I hope he and his son change their mind and I hope the plan goes down as well.

On Saturday, my day off, I was at the Wells Middle School campus at 8:00 am. I walked around the campus where I took before photos of the damage. I planned on taking after photos once the project was complete. I was able to locate all the paint, paint brushes and supplies that the maintenance department provided. Things were looking good. So far, so good.

Around 8:45 am I saw cars pulling into the staff parking lot at the middle school. Inside the cars I saw parents and their sons waiting to start work. By 9:00 am all the parents and all the boys were present. Some of them did not look very excited to be on campus but they were there to work.

I called every one over to the center of the campus and I stood on the steps of the main office so that everyone could see and hear me. I had a list of names and I began with morning roll call.

I called Aaron, Max, Sam, Vincent, Noah, Douglas, Sean, Clint, Dustin, Derik, Brent, Austin, Nathan, Stan, Howard, Ross, Lee, Chandler, Wade and Alan. They were all there and so were the parents. I thought to myself this plan might work.

After student roll call I asked all the boys to walk to a fence while I spoke with their parents. The boys left the area and all that was left were parents.

I told the parents that I knew today was their day off of work, my day off as well, but I needed them to stay with their sons to supervise them. I informed the parents, "If we all worked together we could be done at the end of the day and the juvenile district attorney's office and the school district would be satisfied." I told the parents what kind of work was needed and I assigned parents and their sons with work assignments. As soon as I was done with the assignments the parents were off to start work. Again I thought to myself this might work.

I saw boys with paint brushes, paint cans and everything they needed to repair their school. I walked to the rear area where portable classrooms were and I saw boys painting the portable classroom buildings.

I walked to the school gym area and I saw boys painting the building. I saw a group of boys painting parking stalls in the main campus parking lot and again I saw boys painting everything that appeared to need fresh paint. I saw parents watching their sons work off their mistake. This plan is working.

Once I saw everyone working and about an hour had passed I decided to unlock the restrooms in case someone needed to use the restroom. That's when I saw a possible problem.

I saw a minivan with two moms drive off campus. I walked over to a group of boys painting the parking lot and I asked, "Where are they going?" one boy answered saying "They told us that they were going to be right back." I thought to myself, is my plan falling apart now?

I returned to the restroom and I unlocked them for use.

About twenty minutes later the two moms were back on campus. The two moms had gone to a grocery store and bought all the boys snacks for a break. I saw them with large grocery bags filled with food and drinks. The boys all gathered in the outside cafeteria area and the parents picked up paintbrushes to finish their son's work. Now that is teamwork.

As the boys were taking their snack break a parent walked up to me and asked, "What happened to Kyle and his dad Jim?"

I informed him that Kyle and his dad Jim decided they did not want to participate in the community service project.

I said, "Jim called me and according to him and a neighbor's attorney they did not have to participate." The parents said, "That sounds like Jim. He can be a real hot head because I once played golf with him before and Jim is always looking for a way to get out of things." I ended saying "Jim may be playing golf right now."

When the break was over all the boys went back to work. The project was looking good. Everyone was working real hard to repair his vandalism mess.

About seven hours later the parents reported all repairs and painting had been repaired. The boys were placing their paintbrushes and cleaning gear away and everyone was waiting for me to inspect their work. I grabbed my camera to take after photos.

I was really impressed. The boys painted five portable classrooms, the outdoor area of the school gym had a fresh coat of paint, all the faded paint in the main parking lot stalls was repaired with fresh white paint on every parking stall, all the red curbs had a fresh coat of red paint, the handicap spaces had fresh blue paint, the yellow loading zone curb had a fresh coat of paint and the outdoor asphalt area on the outdoor basketball courts were painted with fresh white paint. The boys and their parents did a lot of work.

I called everyone over to the steps of the main office building and I told everyone "Just look at all the good work you did today. Pat yourselves on the back because your school has a fresh new look and it's all because you and your parents volunteered to make your school better looking." I ended by saying, "When I was a young boy my grandfather gave me some advice to always think about. He said, everyone makes mistakes so learn from your mistakes and don't repeat that same mistake. If you make the same mistake again that is not a mistake. That is you being stupid. I'm not calling you here today stupid but you did correct your mistake and I think you learned from your mistake. Good job everyone."I saw many of the parents and boys smile. Everyone was pleased with the outcome.

I informed all the parents and their sons that I would call the juvenile district attorney and inform him that the community service project was a complete success and I had photos to prove it. I dismissed everyone and I walked over and locked the restrooms.

On Monday morning Principal Sheppard arrived on campus and he too was completely surprised to see all the work the boys did to repair their school campus. Principal Sheppard was now very happy.

When I arrived on campus around 9:30 am I met with Principal Sheppard and his secretary June. Robert had nothing to say but good things about the community service project. I asked Robert if he was willing to write the juvenile district attorney a letter commending the parents and their sons for working hard and for taking the community service project serious. Robert said, "Yes of course, I'll write the letter today." Robert also began calling some of the involved parents to thank them for showing their sons how to take responsibility for their actions and how important it was to respect their school.

I informed Principal Sheppard not to call Kyle or his dad Jim because they chose not to participate. June said, "That figures, Jim always tried to get out of things, even when Kyle's older brother Keith attended middle school and got into trouble, Jim never taught him how to take responsibility for anything."I said, "I will be sending only Kyle's police report to the juvenile court so we'll see what happens."

When I returned to the police station I called the juvenile district attorney and I gave him an update on the community service project at Wells Middle School. I informed him that Kyle and his dad Jim did not attend as they first promised.

199

I informed him that, "Jim called me the day before the community service project was to start and according to Jim he spoke with a neighbor that knows an attorney and he learned he did not have to participate." The juvenile district attorney said to just send the police report and we will see what happens.

Over a week went by and one day I was visiting the Wells Middle School campus when three boys ran up to me. It was Sean, Brent and Chandler. Three of the boys who had participated in the community service project.

They were pretty excited and they asked me "Did you hear about what happened to Kyle?"I said, "No, is he all right? They went on to say, "This is what happened." The boys were eager to speak but Brent said, "We heard Kyle and his dad went to Juvenile Court and Kyle was found guilty of felony vandalism." Chandler said, "Yeah, and Kyle has to do eight weeks of community service in Oakland and be on juvenile probation for three years." Sean asked, "Does that mean Kyle will have a felony record for the rest of his life?" Brent and Chandler said, "Kyle is stupid."

I tried to correct the boys and I told them "Kyle is not stupid, Kyle and his dad had some bad advice and maybe they should have thought things over before they learned the hard way."

The boys left me to talk with some of their other school friends. I saw them laughing as they walked away. Maybe I should call Kyle's dad and give him some of my grandfather's wise advice.

Another case solved by good supportive parents, a strong Dublin community and their SRO

ABOOKS

ALIVE Book Publishing and ALIVE Publishing Group
are imprints of Advanced Publishing LLC,
3200 A Danville Blvd., Suite 204, Alamo, California 94507

Telephone: 925.837.7303 Fax: 925.837.6951
www.alivebookpublishing.com

CPSIA information can be obtained
at www.ICGtesting.com
Printed in the USA
LVOW11s0441200617
538610LV00001B/99/P